Jo Seagar
cooks

Jo Seagar
COOKS

Photography by Jae Frew

RANDOM HOUSE
NEW ZEALAND

To Fanny Gray

ACKNOWLEDGEMENTS

A big thank you to Jae and Jo Frew for fabulous photographs and great style; to Karyn, Sean and Rose; Maree O'Neill; Annuh Ngatai; Kate, Guy and Ross Seagar; James Ball; Phil and all the wonderful staff at Seagars Oxford — thank you very much; and especially to Jenny Hellen at Random House, for her wise counsel.

A catalogue record for this book is available from the National Library of New Zealand

A RANDOM HOUSE BOOK
published by
Random House New Zealand
18 Poland Road, Glenfield, Auckland, New Zealand
www.randomhouse.co.nz

First published 2006. Reprinted 2006

ISBN-13: 978 1 86941 814 4
ISBN-10: 1 86941 814 X

Cover and text design: Trevor Newman
Cover photographs: Jae Frew
Printed in China

CONTENTS

I like the idea of slow food, if it's the description of the opposite of fast food. I don't mind if a dish takes ages to cook as long as I don't have to stand by and stir for that length of time.

Introduction

Easy entertaining may seem like a contradiction in terms but, believe me, creating relaxed and memorable events is very achievable. Eating at home, you just know you're going to get a good table — the best in the house, in fact.

I love to cook for and entertain people at home, but I'm not prepared to lay down my life for the cause. All that preparation and fluffing about from Tuesday, getting ready for Saturday night, is just not me.

I want quick, short recipes using readily available ingredients. I want to measure things with cups and spoons, not have to drag out weights and scales to measure 183 g of flour or 7 g of dried yeast.

'Minimum effort for maximum effect' is my personal motto. 'Easy peasy' is the corollary — I even have the number plates (how do you retrain a husband to think in terms of jewellery for gifts?).

The pace of change in the world is so fast people like to cling to the familiar, particularly with their food. Heritage is the new vintage, but I refuse to be hidebound by tradition just for the sake of it. I've lightened recipes and pared them down, especially in their methodology. If I can ditch the sifting and creaming butter and sugar steps I have, and rethought the presentation. Guests will think you've gone to lots of extra effort if you make individual servings of established favourites like sticky puds and crusty pies. A number of these recipes are my personal interpretations of traditional dishes, with the intelligent use of good, ready-prepared products.

This book is about creating the right food at the right time, and sharing it with the people you love.

I want you to put flowers back on the table, think of the hen that laid your egg, and remember your mother and put on an apron — it's not demeaning, it's there to keep your clothes clean.

The great gift of appetite is that there is always something new and fresh to savour.

Happy cooking, my friends.

Jo Seagar

1 BREAKFAST, BRUNCH & MORNING FOOD

Banana Bread

A loaf that slices easily without crumbling, yet stays nice and moist and freezes well. Perfect for morning tea or in a lunch box, spread with cream cheese, butter or peanut butter.

125 g butter or margarine, softened
1 cup sugar
2 eggs
3 soft, over-ripe bananas, mashed with a fork
1½ cups flour
1 teaspoon baking soda
½ teaspoon salt

Makes 1 standard loaf
Preheat oven to 180°C. Spray a standard 23 x 12 cm (6-cup capacity) loaf tin with non-stick baking spray and line with baking paper.

Beat the softened butter and sugar until creamy and pale. Beat in the eggs, then the mashed banana. Gently mix in the flour, baking soda and salt and when just combined, pour into the prepared tin.

Bake for approximately 1 hour, until the loaf is springy in the centre and has pulled away from the sides of the tin. Cool in the tin and slice when cold. Wrap in cling film or tinfoil to freeze.

Instant Banana Berry Frozen Yoghurt

Low fat and really delicious — the secret is the frozen berries.

2 large, ripe bananas
2-3 tablespoons caster sugar, to taste
500 g mixed frozen berries (blueberries, raspberries etc)
2 cups low-fat yoghurt, plain or berry flavoured, well chilled

Serves 2–3
Slice the bananas into a food processor and whiz with the sugar and berries. When the mixture is nice and smooth but still very icy, add the yoghurt and mix until just combined. Serve immediately.

Lemon Crust Blueberry Muffins

A lovely café-style muffin with a drizzle of sharp lemon curd to complement the sweet, crusty blueberry taste — and it's quick to make.

1 egg
¼ cup oil (lite olive,
    canola or
    rice-bran oil)
1 cup milk
¾ cup sugar
grated rind of 1 lemon
2 tablespoons lemon juice
2 cups flour

4 teaspoons baking powder
1 cup blueberries (if using
    frozen, do not defrost)
½ cup Lemon Curd to serve

FOR THE TOPPING
50 g butter, melted
1 tablespoon lemon juice
¼ cup caster sugar

Makes 12

Preheat oven to 180°C. Spray a 12-muffin tray with non-stick baking spray.

Mix the egg, oil, milk, sugar, lemon rind and juice together in a large bowl until well combined. Add the flour, baking powder and blueberries and mix until just folded in. Do not over-mix. It does not matter if there is still a little flour visible. Spoon the mixture into the prepared muffin tray and bake for 30–35 minutes.

Whisk the melted butter and lemon juice together. Remove tray from the oven and brush the hot muffins with the butter and lemon mixture, then sprinkle generously with caster sugar. Leave in the tray until cool enough to handle, then remove to cool further on a wire rack. Serve with the tops dug out and a teaspoon of lemon curd poured in. Place the little top back on like a hat.

Lemon Curd

4 large, juicy lemons
4 eggs, beaten

2 cups sugar
200 g butter

Makes about 2½ cups

Wash the lemons then finely grate the rind and squeeze the juice into a small saucepan. Add the beaten eggs, sugar and butter cut up into little cubes.

Stir constantly with a wire whisk over very gentle heat until the sugar dissolves and the mixture thickens. Keep the heat very low and don't be tempted to speed it up or to stop stirring. Pour into a plastic container and store in the fridge.

Healthy Raisin Loaf

This is great buttered and it can be toasted too.
Good if there's no bread in the house.

1 cup rolled oats
1 cup bran
2 cups raisins, or substitute other
    dried fruit (sultanas, apricots etc)
2 cups raw sugar
2 cups milk
2 cups self-raising flour

Makes 1 large loaf
Preheat oven to 150°C. Grease or spray a large loaf tin with non-stick
baking spray.
    Soak the rolled oats, bran, raisins and sugar in the milk for 10 minutes. Stir
in the flour and spoon into the tin. Bake for 1½ hours. Cool on a wire rack.

Avocado and Cucumber Smoothie

5 chive stalks, plus a chive flower
1 avocado, halved
1 small Lebanese or ⅓ telegraph cucumber
5 tablespoons sweetened natural yoghurt,
    or fromage frais
grated rind and juice of 2 limes
salt and freshly ground black pepper
Tabasco sauce to taste

Makes 2 glasses
Chop the chives finely, reserving 1 teaspoon plus the chive flower and placing the
rest into a blender. Scoop the avocado flesh into the blender. Peel and chop up
the cucumber and add to the blender. Add the yoghurt, lime rind and juice, and
a good measure of seasoning and Tabasco sauce to taste. Whiz until creamy and
smooth. Taste and check seasoning before pouring into glasses to serve. Sprinkle
the reserved chives and petals of the chive flower over the top. If desired, the
mixture can be thinned with trim milk.

Breakfast Spuddy Fry-up

This is everybody's favourite weekend breakfast in the Seagar family and usually means we need to have tatties in the pot the night before.

8–10 large, cold, boiled potatoes,
   in their skins
2 tablespoons oil
25 g butter
½ teaspoon garlic salt
1 tablespoon chopped parsley
½ cup grated Parmesan cheese

Serves 6

Roughly slice the cold potatoes. Heat the oil and butter in a large non-stick frypan and add the sliced potatoes. Pan-fry until golden brown. Toss in the garlic salt, parsley and grated Parmesan and cook a few minutes more, until the cheese melts. For a totally decadent brunch, add a ½ cup of cream with the Parmesan and cook until it bubbles.

Italian-style One-dish Brunch

6 spicy Italian sausages

1–2 teaspoons oil

6 slices thickly cut (2 cm) ciabatta or
  French bread, cut into cubes

1 cup cherry tomatoes

1 handful small basil leaves

1 cup grated tasty cheese

¾ cup grated Parmesan cheese

8 eggs

¾ cup milk

¼ cup chopped parsley

salt and freshly ground black pepper

Serves 4–6

Preheat oven to 200°C.

Pan-fry sausages in a non-stick ovenproof pan with a little oil until browned and cooked right through. Drain sausages on paper towels and chop into chunky bite-sized pieces.

Wipe out excess oil from the pan with paper towels. Place the sausage pieces, bread cubes and cherry tomatoes in the pan and sprinkle the basil leaves and grated cheeses over the top.

Beat the eggs, milk and parsley together, seasoning generously with salt and pepper. Pour this egg mixture over the pan ingredients, stirring just a little to evenly distribute the liquid. Bake for 25–30 minutes until puffed up and golden brown. Cut into portions with a spatula to serve.

Brunch is a classic way to entertain family and friends, probably because it accommodates so many tastes and ages.

Vanilla French Toast

Another perfect brunch favourite, great served with crispy bacon and maple syrup.

4 eggs
100 ml milk
salt and finely ground white pepper
½ teaspoon vanilla essence
1 teaspoon caster sugar
8 slices French bread, approximately 1.5 cm thick
lite olive oil for cooking
25 g butter, cut into cubes
icing sugar to dust
maple syrup or fruit purée to serve

Serves 4

Whisk eggs, milk, salt, pepper, vanilla essence and caster sugar together. Lay bread in a lasagne dish and pour the egg and milk mixture over to coat well. Turn bread slices to soak up all the mixture.

Heat a large frypan or flat griddle plate on medium heat. Brush with the oil and sizzle a little butter on top. Place French toast on the sizzling butter, cooking about 3–4 minutes until golden brown. Turn and cook the other side. Dust with icing sugar and serve immediately with maple syrup or fruit purée.

Breakfast Trifles

6 fruity muffins (blueberry,
   lemon etc), either homemade or
   bought from the supermarket or bakery
6 tablespoons pure fruit juice
   (orange, mango, pineapple etc)
1 x 500 ml carton prepared dairy custard
1 cup mixed berries, fresh or thawed
1 cup toasted muesli
1 cup thick natural fruit yoghurt

Makes 6

Break muffins into 3 or 4 pieces. In six small ramekins or water glasses build up layers of muffin sprinkled with juice, custard, berries, muesli and yoghurt. Serve well chilled, with teaspoons or parfait spoons.

Creamy Coconut Rice Pudding

Why not serve this classic dessert as a breakfast food? It is great with stewed fruit or fresh tropical fruits.

1 cup arborio or short-grain rice
200 g (½ can) sweetened condensed milk
1 cup coconut cream
3 cups full-cream milk
½ cup cream
¼ cup desiccated coconut
½ teaspoon coconut essence

Serves 4–6

Place all the ingredients, except the coconut essence, in a medium-sized saucepan and bring to the boil, stirring. Reduce temperature to a simmer and keep stirring every now and then for 30 minutes, until the rice is well cooked and thick and creamy textured. Stir in the coconut essence and divide into individual bowls. Chill before serving.

Traditional dishes given a fresh contemporary flavour.

2 SOUPS & MIDDAY FOOD

Chicken, Lime and Orzo Soup

¾ cup orzo (rice-shaped pasta)
1 tablespoon oil
1 onion, peeled and finely chopped
2–3 cloves garlic, crushed (about 1 teaspoon)
1 small red chilli, seeded and thinly sliced
1 chicken breast, sliced into thin fingers
6 cups chicken stock
grated rind and juice of 3 limes
2 large tomatoes, seeded and chopped into pieces
salt and freshly ground black pepper
2 tablespoons fresh chopped coriander
lime wedges to garnish

Serves 4

Cook the orzo in a medium-sized saucepan of boiling water for about 5 minutes, until tender. Drain.

Heat oil in the orzo saucepan. Add the onion, garlic and chilli. Cook, stirring, for 3–4 minutes to soften. Add the chicken strips and stir for 2–3 minutes over the heat.

Add the stock, lime juice and rind and tomato. Simmer until the chicken is well cooked through. Add the orzo and season with salt and pepper.

To serve, ladle into noodle bowls and garnish with chopped coriander and lime wedges.

Butter Chicken Chowder

2 cooked chicken breasts, boneless and skinless
1 tablespoon oil
5 spring onions, sliced
1 cup sliced mushrooms
1–2 tablespoons tandoori paste
1 x 400 g can cream-style sweetcorn
1 litre chicken stock
½ cup sour cream or thick yoghurt
¼ cup fresh chopped coriander
salt and freshly ground black pepper
pappadums or naan bread to serve

Serves 4

Shred the cooked chicken meat and set aside. Heat the oil in a medium-sized saucepan and add the spring onions and mushrooms. Stir-fry for 2–3 minutes until softened. Stir in the tandoori paste and sweetcorn, then the chicken stock and shredded chicken meat. Bring to the boil then reduce heat. Stir in the sour cream or yoghurt and the fresh coriander, seasoning to taste with salt and pepper. Serve with pappadums or naan bread.

This is food in a flash that's full of flavour

Bacon, Corn and Wild Rice Chowder

6 cups chicken stock
1 cup wild rice
6 cups sweetcorn kernels, frozen or canned
1 cup water
2 tablespoons oil
8 rashers rindless smoky bacon, chopped
2 carrots, peeled and diced
2 onions, peeled and chopped
2 cups cream and milk mixed
    (or 1 cup milk and 1 cup cream)
½ cup chopped parsley
salt and freshly ground black pepper

Serves 6

Bring chicken stock to the boil in a large saucepan. Add the wild rice, reduce heat and simmer for 15 minutes. In a food processor or blender mix half the corn and 1 cup of water to a smooth purée.

Heat oil in a frypan. Add the bacon and cook until crisp. Add the carrot and onion and cook for 5 minutes. Mix all the ingredients, including the remaining corn, in the saucepan and simmer for 10–15 minutes. Season generously with salt and pepper.

Minestrone-style 'Escape to the Country' Soup

An easy minestrone-style soup that cheats because you open a few cans rather than prepare everything from scratch but hey — it's simple, quick and so warming.

2–3 cloves garlic, crushed
(about 1 teaspoon)
3 spring onions, sliced
1 onion, peeled and chopped
2 tablespoons olive oil
2 x 400 g cans chopped
tomatoes in juice
4 tomato-cans water
2 teaspoons chicken or
vegetable stock powder
2 tablespoons basil pesto

1 cup dried small pasta
(risoni or macaroni)
1 x 400 g can white beans, drained
1 cup frozen peas
1 cup frozen corn
4 spicy chorizo sausages, sliced
1 tablespoon Worcestershire sauce
1 cup chopped parsley
salt and freshly ground
black pepper
grated Parmesan cheese to serve

Serves 4–6

Fry the garlic, spring onions and onion in the oil for 3–4 minutes to soften. Add the tomatoes and juice, plus 4 tomato-cans of water, the stock powder and pesto. Bring to the boil and add the pasta and white beans. Cook for about 8 minutes until the pasta is soft. Add the peas, corn, sausages, Worcestershire sauce and parsley. Check the seasoning — remember the Worcestershire sauce is quite spicy. Add salt and freshly ground black pepper to taste and serve. A good grating of fresh Parmesan over this dish is delicious.

Use this recipe as a blueprint for a quick but substantial soup, adding cold chicken, roast vegetables, herbs etc as desired.

Try floating little toasted garlic breads on the top.

Roast Carrot and Fresh Ginger Soup

6 large carrots, peeled and cut into chunks
2 medium onions, peeled and quartered
5 cloves garlic, unpeeled and whole
1 tablespoon olive oil
2 cups vegetable or chicken stock
2 teaspoons grated fresh ginger
salt and freshly ground black pepper
2 tablespoons toasted flaked almonds
4 slices Japanese pickled ginger to garnish

Serves 4–6

Preheat oven to 200°C.

Place the carrot chunks, onion quarters and garlic in a roasting tin and drizzle with olive oil. Stir to coat well. Roast for 35–40 minutes until the carrots are tender and browned. Place the carrot and onion in a blender, with the garlic squeezed out of its skin, plus the stock and fresh ginger. Purée until smooth. Rewarm in a saucepan, adding salt and pepper to taste. Serve sprinkled with almonds and pickled ginger.

Quality of life is not about sacrifice or starvation; it's about a sense of well-being.

Smoked Salmon on Potato Rosti

6 medium potatoes (Ilam Hardy are good)
2 tablespoons oil
250 g spreadable (could be lite) cream cheese
1 tablespoon chopped chives
1 tablespoon chopped parsley
1 tablespoon lemon juice
½ teaspoon grated lemon rind
salt and freshly ground black pepper
150 g smoked salmon, sliced
4 teaspoons caviar or smoked salmon roe
watercress sprigs to garnish

Serves 4

Peel and grate the potatoes onto a clean tea-towel. Squeeze out as much excess liquid as possible.

Heat the oil in a frypan and, using a spatula, flatten piles of potato, cooking until golden brown and crisp. Drain on paper towels and keep warm as you cook the whole batch.

Mix the cream cheese with the herbs, lemon juice and rind, and salt and pepper. To serve, layer potato rosti, cheese mixture and smoked salmon in a double stack on each plate, garnished with a teaspoon of caviar and a sprig of watercress.

Roast Chicken and Sesame Asparagus Salad

1 roasted or rotisserie-grilled chicken
1 handful mung bean sprouts
1 bag (2–3 handfuls) baby spinach leaves
5 spring onions, thinly sliced
2 handfuls thin asparagus,
   sliced into bite-sized pieces
 2 oranges, peeled and divided into segments

FOR THE DRESSING
1 tablespoon toasted sesame seeds
1 tablespoon black sesame seeds
juice and grated rind of 3 oranges
2 tablespoons tahini paste or
   crunchy peanut butter
½ cup chopped parsley
1 teaspoon sesame oil

Serves 4

Remove all the meat from the chicken (reserving the bones for stock). Place the chicken, bean sprouts, spinach leaves and spring onion in a salad bowl. Bring a frypan of water to the boil and toss in the asparagus. Cook for 2 minutes, then drain and refresh under cold water. Add the asparagus and orange segments to the salad.

Make the dressing by placing the sesame seeds, orange juice and rind, tahini paste, parsley and sesame oil in a bowl. Whisk together. Add a little hot water if the dressing is too thick.

Drizzle the dressing over the salad and toss to combine.

Chicken Caesar Salad Wraps

All the components of the classic Caesar salad, folded in flour tortilla wraps for easy handling.

FOR THE CAESAR DRESSING
1 egg yolk
juice and grated rind of 1 small lemon
1 teaspoon Worcestershire sauce
150 ml olive oil
½ cup grated or shaved Parmesan cheese
salt and freshly ground black pepper
2–3 tablespoons boiling water

FOR THE SALAD
3 rashers rindless streaky bacon
2 cooked chicken breasts
6 soft flour tortillas
1 small cos lettuce, shredded
*   (about 3 cups)*
6 anchovy fillets in oil,
*   drained and chopped*
½ cup Parmesan cheese,
*   shaved with a potato peeler*

Serves 6

To make the dressing, place the egg yolk, lemon juice and rind and Worcestershire sauce in a blender. While running the machine, add the olive oil slowly then add the Parmesan, salt and pepper. Thin the dressing with 2–3 tablespoons of boiling water to a pourable consistency.

Fry the bacon until crisp and drain on paper towels before crumbling. Shred the chicken with two forks.

Lay the tortillas flat on a bench. Arrange lettuce down the centre. Top with chicken, bacon, anchovies and Parmesan and drizzle with dressing. Roll up and wrap in a napkin to serve.

Thai-style Mussels

2 kg fresh mussels
1 tablespoon olive oil
2–3 cloves garlic, crushed (about 1 teaspoon)
1 red chilli, deseeded and finely sliced
1 teaspoon crushed lemongrass stalk
  (white part only)
1 large bunch coriander, leaves removed and
  stalks finely chopped
1 x 400 ml can coconut cream
300 ml chicken or fish stock
salt and freshly ground black pepper

Serves 4

Scrub the mussels with a stiff brush, such as a nail brush, and pull off any hairy
beards. Discard any mussels that are open and rinse the rest well under cold
running water. In a large lidded saucepan heat the oil then add the garlic, chilli,
lemongrass and chopped coriander stalks. Cook for 2–3 minutes, stirring. Add
the coconut cream, stock and salt and pepper. Bring to the boil then adjust heat
to a gentle simmer. Add the mussels, cover the saucepan and cook for 5 minutes.

Tip the mussels into a colander placed over a bowl to catch the liquid.
Discard any unopened mussels and divide the remainder between 4 serving
bowls. Pour the liquid over the top and garnish with coriander leaves. Serve with
crusty bread for dipping in the sauce.

If you enjoyed making it, your friends will enjoy eating it.

Cheesy Tuna and Broccoli Bake

Even 'cheap-as-chips' processed foods can be key ingredients in a great home-cooked meal.

1 x 400 g packet pasta (penne or ziti)
1 medium-sized head broccoli, broken into florets
1–2 cans tuna in brine (approximately 250 g)
1 cup sliced button mushrooms
1 x 400 g can mushroom soup
150 ml milk
1 cup grated tasty cheese
1 small packet natural potato chips

Serves 4

Preheat oven to 200°C. Spray an ovenproof casserole or large, deep lasagne dish with non-stick baking spray.

Boil the pasta in a large saucepan of salted water until tender. Add the broccoli for the last 3 minutes of cooking time. Drain well and tip into the prepared dish. Drain the tuna and flake it over the broccoli and pasta. Sprinkle the sliced mushrooms over the top. Mix the soup and milk together and pour over, gently stirring to mix. Sprinkle with the cheese and crush the potato chips over the top.

Bake for 15–20 minutes until the topping is crispy and golden and the dish is well heated through.

Penne and Portobellos

3 medium onions, peeled and chopped
1 tablespoon butter
2 tablespoons olive oil
1 teaspoon sugar
1 tablespoon olive oil
500 g portobello mushrooms, sliced
   (approximately 8 large mushrooms)
1 handful flat-leaf Italian parsley, chopped
salt and freshly ground black pepper
500 g penne pasta
½ cup shaved Parmesan cheese
1-2 tablespoons extra virgin olive oil to serve

Serves 4

Place onions, butter, 2 tablespoons oil and sugar in a large sauté pan and cook over medium heat, stirring frequently until browned and caramelised (about 20–25 minutes). Transfer to a bowl. Heat 1 tablespoon olive oil in the pan and stir- fry the mushrooms until tender and browned (about 10 minutes). Add the onion mixture and the parsley and season to taste with salt and pepper.

In a large saucepan of boiling salted water, cook the penne until just tender. Drain, reserving 1 cup of the pasta water. Toss the drained pasta into the mushroom mixture and toss with the reserved pasta water and Parmesan. Drizzle with extra virgin olive oil just prior to serving. Serve with a green salad and crusty bread.

Children will not remember you for the material things you provided. They won't be able to recall the list of Christmas gifts. But they will remember the cast of characters present and the feeling that you cherished them.

Avocado and Prawn Salad with Lime Coriander Dressing

FOR THE DRESSING
2 tablespoons olive oil
2 tablespoons fresh lime juice
2 tablespoons chopped coriander
2 tablespoons cold water
1 tablespoon Asian fish sauce
1 teaspoon brown sugar
1–2 cloves garlic, crushed (about ½ teaspoon)

FOR THE SALAD
300–500 g cooked peeled prawns (I've used
  ones with their tails still on)
2 firm but ripe avocados, peeled and sliced
1 punnet cherry tomatoes, halved (about 2 cups)
1 handful blanched, peeled broad beans
  or green beans
2 handfuls mixed salad leaves or mesclun
1 handful roughly chopped or sprigged parsley

Serves 6
Mix all dressing ingredients in a screw-top jar or mini blender.

Mix the salad ingredients on a large flat platter or in a shallow bowl. Keep cold in the fridge under a damp tea-towel until ready to serve. Either drizzle the dressing over the salad or pass it around separately.

Throw-it-together Self-crusting Pie

This is one of those seemingly impossibly easy quiche thingies where you throw it all in together. A great recipe when you're in a hurry.

4 eggs, beaten
1½ cups grated tasty cheese
1 small onion, peeled and chopped
6 rashers rindless bacon, chopped
½ cup self-raising flour
1½ cups milk
¼ cup chopped parsley
salt and freshly ground black pepper
2 cups of your choice of chopped mushrooms,
    peppers, cherry tomatoes, courgettes, corn,
    peas, beans, grated pumpkin etc

Serves 6

Preheat oven to 180°C. Spray a medium- to large-sized lasagne dish with non-stick baking spray.

Mix all the ingredients in a bowl. Pour into the prepared dish and bake for 40–45 minutes until set and golden brown.

Style is manners, confidence, and simplicity.

Hazelnut, Pumpkin and Blue Cheese Fritters

4 eggs
1 cup self-raising flour
1 cup grated raw pumpkin
½ cup chopped hazelnuts
½ cup finely chopped or
*   crumbled blue cheese*
½ cup chopped parsley
salt and freshly ground black pepper
½ cup oil and 50g butter to cook
extra chopped hazelnuts and
*   hollandaise sauce to serve*

Makes about 10 fritters

In a bowl, beat the eggs. Mix in the flour to produce a smooth batter (this can be done in a food processor or with an electric mixer). Add the pumpkin, hazelnuts, blue cheese, parsley and salt and pepper to taste.

Heat the oil and butter in a pan over medium heat until bubbly. Spoon 2–3 fritters into the pan and cook for approximately 3 minutes, then carefully turn and cook the other side. Drain the fritters on paper towels and keep them warm in the oven while you cook the remaining mixture.

These fritters are great served with hollandaise sauce and a few chopped hazelnuts.

3 BAKING, AFTERNOON TEA & FILLING THE TINS

Devonshire Tea Pikelets

So easy to make (easier than scones, I think) and what a treat, especially for a smart afternoon tea when you've got out the best cups.

1 teaspoon baking soda
1 cup milk
1 egg
3 tablespoons white sugar
2 cups flour
2 teaspoons cream of tartar
whipped cream or thick yoghurt and
*   jam to serve*
fruit or berries to garnish

Makes about 20

Dissolve the baking soda in the milk.

Beat the egg and sugar, then mix in the flour and cream of tartar. Add the milk and mix to a smooth batter, using a little extra milk if required. (I use a blender for mixing the batter.) Spoon onto a heated, non-stick or well-greased heavy frypan or crêpe pan.

Cook over a medium heat until bubbles appear on top and the undersurface is golden brown. Turn and cook the other side. Don't have the pan too hot.

Cool on a wire rack while you cook the rest of the batch. Serve with a little dollop of whipped cream or thick yoghurt and jam and perhaps some berries or pieces of fresh fruit to garnish.

Vanilla Peanut Blondies

A family favourite biscuit: a big vanilla taste in a pale, nutty cookie — like a blonde version of a peanut brownie.

300 g butter
1 cup sugar
2 teaspoons vanilla essence
2 cups self-raising flour
2 cups shelled roasted peanuts,
  or use salted peanuts

Makes 36

Preheat oven to 180°C.

In a bowl, beat the butter and sugar together until creamy. Add the vanilla essence, flour and peanuts. Place teaspoonfuls of the mixture onto a tray lined with baking paper, leaving each room to spread. Bake for 15 minutes. Allow to cool for a few minutes on the tray before removing to a wire rack. Store in an airtight container.

Cappuccino Date Slice

2 eggs

1 cup brown sugar

180 g butter, melted

½ cup milk

2 tablespoons sweetened coffee and
   chicory essence (available in the
   coffee section of the supermarket)

1 cup dates, pitted and chopped into small pieces

1½ cups flour

2 teaspoons baking powder

FOR THE COFFEE ICING

2 cups icing sugar

1 tablespoon sweetened coffee and
   chicory essence

25 g butter, melted

boiling water

Makes 30 pieces

Preheat oven to 150°C. Spray a 20 x 30 cm slice tin with non-stick baking spray and line the base with baking paper.

Beat the eggs in a large bowl, add all other ingredients and mix well to combine thoroughly. Spread into the prepared tin and bake for 30 minutes. Cool in the tin. When cold, spread with coffee icing.

For the coffee icing, mix all the ingredients together, adding enough boiling water to form a smooth, glossy, spreadable icing. Cut when the icing has set.

Raspberry Friands

You can use standard-sized muffin tins if you don't have friand moulds.

175 g butter
1 cup ground almonds
1½ cups icing sugar
½ cup flour
5 egg whites
1 teaspoon raspberry essence
1 cup fresh or frozen raspberries

Makes 8–10 friands

Preheat oven to 220°C. Spray a tray of friand moulds with non-stick baking spray.

Either in the microwave or in a small saucepan, melt the butter, then allow it to cool. Place the ground almonds, icing sugar and flour in a mixing bowl. Add the unbeaten egg whites and mix together. Add the melted butter and raspberry essence and mix well. Spoon approximately a tablespoon of mixture into each greased mould. Place a few raspberries in each friand then cover with the remaining mixture. Bake for 5 minutes, then turn the oven down to 200°C and bake a further 12–15 minutes. Cool in the tins for 5 minutes before carefully turning out onto a wire rack to cool.

Triple-chocolate Rolled-oat Biscuits

250 g butter
¾ cup sugar
3 tablespoons sweetened condensed
    milk (using a tube of condensed
    milk makes this operation a lot easier)
½ teaspoon vanilla essence

1½ cups rolled oats
1½ cups flour
1 teaspoon baking powder
¾ cup each chopped white,
    dark and milk chocolate
    buttons

Makes 30

Preheat oven to 170°C. Spray two oven trays with non-stick baking spray, then line with non-stick baking paper. (Spraying first helps the paper stay in place.)

Beat the butter and sugar until creamy. Add the condensed milk and beat until pale and smooth. Mix in the vanilla, oats, flour and baking powder, then the chocolate chips.

Place spoonfuls of the mixture on the prepared trays and press flat with a wet fork. Bake for 25–30 minutes until golden brown. Cool for 2–3 minutes on the tray, then cool fully on a wire rack. Store in an airtight container.

Indulgent Chocolate Fudge Brownie

If you like a fudgey, gooey, rich, dark chocolate brownie, not at all like chocolate cake, then this is the recipe for you.

200 g butter, melted
¾ cup cocoa
2 cups caster sugar
¼ teaspoon salt
4 eggs

1 teaspoon vanilla essence
¾ cup flour
½ teaspoon baking powder
2 cups chopped chocolate
    or chocolate chips

Makes 18 pieces

Preheat oven to 150°C. Spray a 20 x 30 cm sponge-roll tin with non-stick baking spray and line with non-stick baking paper.

Mix the melted butter, cocoa, sugar, salt, eggs and vanilla essence until well combined, beating until the colour lightens (about 4–5 minutes). Gently mix in the flour, baking powder and chopped chocolate. Pour into the prepared tin and bake for 50–55 minutes. The brownie should still be quite soft in the middle, but will have cracked slightly and pulled away from the edge of the tin. Cool completely in the tin. Cut when cold and store in an airtight container.

Great produce and a darn simple recipe — the best dishes incorporate these two things and it takes great confidence to realise it.

Fresh Bay and Manuka Honey Cake

A delicious syrup-soaked cake perfect for afternoon tea or as a dessert served with thick yoghurt and fruit. Every time we make this cake, the smell of simmering honey attracts bees inside the house.

FOR THE SYRUP
1 cup caster sugar
½ cup manuka honey
1 cup water
juice and grated rind
   of 2 lemons
6 fresh bay leaves
10–12 thin lemon slices,
   pips removed (this will
   probably require
   2 extra lemons)

FOR THE CAKE
3½ cups self-raising flour
1¼ cups ground almonds
1½ cups caster sugar
½ teaspoon salt
grated rind of 1 lemon
200 ml lite olive oil, or other lite oil
½ cup thick natural yoghurt
2 eggs
cream, yoghurt, butter icing or lemon curd
fresh bay leaves to garnish

Serves 6–8

Place the caster sugar, honey and water in a small saucepan and stir over a low heat until the sugar dissolves. Add the lemon juice and rind and the bay leaves. Simmer for 10 minutes. Add the lemon slices and allow to cool completely while you prepare the cake.

Preheat oven to 180°C. Spray 2 x 21 cm spring-form tins with non-stick baking spray and line the bottoms with non-stick baking paper.

Place the flour, almonds, caster sugar, salt and lemon rind in a large bowl. In a blender mix the oil, yoghurt and eggs. Fold into the flour mixture and divide between the prepared tins. Bake for 45–50 minutes.

Turn the cakes onto a wire rack over a roasting tray. Strain the syrup, reserving the lemon slices but discarding the bay leaves. Spoon or brush the syrup over the hot cakes, letting it all be absorbed. The cakes can be sandwiched together with cream, yoghurt, butter icing or lemon curd. Garnish with a few fresh bay leaves and the reserved lemon slices.

Clove and Cinnamon Apple Cake

This is an easy apple cake, rich with spices, that makes the whole house smell like apple pie.

150 g butter
1 x 500 g can apple-pie filling, or
 2 big cups firm stewed apple (not too wet)
1 cup brown sugar
2 eggs
2 cups flour
2 teaspoons ground cinnamon
1 teaspoon ground cloves
2 teaspoons baking powder
½ cup raisins
½ cup walnuts or pecans (optional)
icing sugar to dust
whipped cream or yoghurt to serve (optional)

Preheat oven to 160°C. Spray a 20–21 cm spring-form tin or bundt tin with non-stick baking spray and, if using a spring-form tin, line the base with baking paper.

Place the butter in a large microwave-proof bowl and melt. Then add all the other ingredients and mix well. Pour into the prepared tin and bake for 55–60 minutes. The surface will be golden brown and firm and the edges will be pulling away from the side of the tin.

Cool on a wire rack and dust with icing sugar to serve. It can be served warm as a dessert with softly whipped cream or yoghurt.

Mrs Button's Billy Sponge

This would obviously have originally been made in a billy suspended over a fire or in a coal range, but I've adapted it for a baking in a non-stick loaf tin in a modern oven.

¼ cup sugar
4 eggs
1 cup sugar
1 cup flour
½ teaspoon baking powder

Makes a large loaf — approximately 20 slices
Preheat oven to 180°C. Spray a large 8–10-cup loaf tin, preferably non stick, with non-stick baking spray. Dust the tin with the ¼ cup sugar, shaking out any excess that doesn't stick to the surface.

Beat the eggs and 1 cup sugar with an electric mixer until very thick and pale. Mix in the flour and baking powder and pour into the greased and sugared tin. Sprinkle a little extra sugar over the surface and bake for 30–35 minutes until well risen and rather cracked on the top.

Cool on a wire rack and slice when cold. The texture is quite chewy. The cake lasts 2–3 days stored in an airtight container. It makes a great dessert base, topped with fruit and ice cream, or it can be grilled or toasted.

Pecan-Parsnip Passion Cake

An interesting new take on a luxury carrot cake, with pecans and spices and a fluffy ginger cream-cheese frosting.

FOR THE CAKE
1½ cups flour
1 cup brown sugar
1 tablespoon ground ginger
2 teaspoons baking powder
2 teaspoons ground cinnamon
2 teaspoons mixed spice
3 eggs
½ cup oil (canola or lite olive oil)
½ cup milk
2 teaspoons vanilla essence

2 cups peeled, grated parsnip
(easy to do in a food processor)
3 tablespoons finely chopped
crystallised ginger
¾ cup chopped pecans

FOR THE FROSTING
125 g cream cheese, softened
25 g butter, softened
2 teaspoons ground ginger
3 cups icing sugar (approximately)

Makes 12 generous pieces

Preheat oven to 180°C. Spray a 20 x 30 cm sponge-roll tin with non-stick baking spray and line with baking paper.

Place the flour, brown sugar, ground ginger, baking powder, cinnamon and mixed spice in a large bowl. In a separate bowl, whisk the eggs, oil, milk and vanilla essence, then tip this into the dry ingredients and mix well. Add the parsnip, crystallised ginger and pecans.

Pour into the prepared tin and bake for 25–30 minutes, until firm in the centre and pulling away from the sides of the tin. Cool the cake completely in the tin before frosting.

For the frosting, beat the cream cheese and butter together until fluffy and smoothly combined. Beat in the ginger and enough icing sugar to make a spreadable but firm consistency. Spread over the cake and chill for at least 3 hours to set.

Earl Grey Currant Loaf

1 cup strong, hot tea (Earl Grey,
   of course)
1 cup dried currants

1 cup brown sugar
2 cups self-raising flour
1 egg

Place the tea, currants and brown sugar in a bowl and soak until the tea is
cold — it can be left overnight.

Preheat oven to 180°C. Spray a loaf tin with non-stick baking spray and
line with baking paper.

Mix the flour and egg into the currant mixture. Pour into the prepared tin
and bake for one hour. Cool on a wire rack and serve sliced and buttered.

Big Chocolate Birthday Cake

Terribly easy to make and sure to delight the recipient, with enough slices
for all the gang. A great cake to share with the whole class or team.

FOR THE CAKE
3 cups sugar
3 cups flour
3 teaspoons baking powder
3 teaspoons baking soda
3 eggs
1½ cups sour cream
¾ cup cocoa

1½ cups strong coffee
   (can be made with instant coffee)
2 teaspoons vanilla essence

FOR THE GLAZE
200 g dark chocolate
50 g butter
1 tablespoon golden syrup

Serves 12–14

Preheat oven to 180°C. Spray a large 28–30 cm spring-form
tin with non-stick baking spray and line the base with baking
paper.

Place all the cake ingredients in a food processor or large
mixing bowl and mix well. Pour into the prepared tin and
bake for 70–75 minutes. Cool on a wire rack.

Melt the dark chocolate, butter and golden syrup
together and mix until smooth. Carefully level the top of
the cake with a sharp knife, then spread with the chocolate
glaze. A message can be piped in white chocolate on the top.

'Dark and Stormy Night' Chocolate Almond Cake (Gluten Free)

200 g butter
250 g dark chocolate, chopped
8 eggs (2 whole, 6 separated)
1 cup caster sugar
2 cups ground almonds
1 teaspoon vanilla essence
¾ cup cocoa

2 tablespoons extra caster sugar
cream, yoghurt or ice cream and
    fresh fruit to serve

FOR THE ICING
375 g dark chocolate melts
100 ml cream

Makes at least 10 portions

Preheat oven to 150°C. Line a 23 cm cake tin with non-stick baking paper.

Melt the butter and chocolate together and stir gently to mix. Beat together two whole eggs plus the 6 egg yolks and the cup of caster sugar. Beat until pale and creamy. Mix in the melted butter and chocolate, ground almonds, vanilla essence and cocoa. Beat the 6 egg whites until stiff. Add the 2 tablespoons of caster sugar, beat well, then fold gently into the chocolate mixture. Pour into the prepared tin and bake for 40–45 minutes until just firm in the centre. Cool in the tin. Melt the icing ingredients together, stirring until smooth. Pour over the cooled cake while it is still in the tin. Chill to set the icing, then turn out. Cut with a hot knife, wiping after each slice. Serve with cream, yoghurt or ice cream and fresh fruit.

I get a kick out of friends coming over to eat and demanding second helpings.

Clementine Slice

A delicious citrussy slice that forms a fine meringue layer on top — quite sticky and lick-your-fingers more-ish.

FOR THE BASE
1½ cups flour
¾ cup caster sugar
150 g butter, cut into cubes,
    at room temperature

FOR THE TOPPING
4 eggs
1¾ cups caster sugar
grated rind of 2 lemons
grated rind of 2 oranges
½ cup lemon juice
¼ cup orange juice
⅓ cup flour
icing sugar to dust

Makes 12–16 pieces

Preheat oven to 180°C. Spray a 20 x 30 cm sponge-roll tin with non-stick baking spray and line with baking paper.

Place the base ingredients in a food processor and run the machine until the pastry clumps around the blade. Press the base into the prepared tin and bake for 15 minutes until dry and lightly golden brown.

Without washing the food processor, whiz up the eggs, caster sugar and lemon and orange rind until really frothy. Add the juices and flour and pulse to just combine. Carefully pour over the hot base and return to the oven for 35–40 minutes, until the topping is set. Cool, slice and dust with icing sugar to serve.

4 DRINKS, PARTY NIBBLES & PASS-AROUND FOOD

Summer Punch

One of the best non-alcoholic summer punch recipes. Make it in jugs for easy pouring.

ice
slices of fruit (strawberry, melon, raspberries etc)
mint leaves
1 litre pineapple juice
2 litres Lemon & Paeroa or dry ginger ale

Serves 8–10
Half-fill tall glasses with ice. Add fruit and mint. Mix the pineapple juice and Lemon & Paeroa in a jug and pour into the glasses.

Sparkling Limeade

This is very refreshing on a summer's day and a lovely non-alcoholic drink that dresses up smartly for a drinks or cocktail party.

3 cups sugar
1 cup fresh lime juice
*   (8–10 limes)*
2 teaspoons grated lime rind
2 teaspoons citric acid
3 cups water
sparkling mineral water or
*   soda water to serve*
crushed ice, mint sprigs and
*   lime slices to serve*

Makes 30 servings
In a saucepan over medium heat, combine sugar, lime juice and rind, citric acid and water. Stir to dissolve. Store in an airtight bottle.

To serve, use 1 part cordial to 5–6 parts sparkling mineral water or soda water, with crushed ice, mint sprigs and lime slices to garnish.

Making use of ready-made ingredients is a great time-saver, and the true art of cooking is knowing which corners to cut without compromising on taste. It's how to cheat with a flourish.

Warm Spiced Wine

There is nothing better than a warming glass of wine après ski, or after a cold winter's hike.

½ cup brown sugar
grated rind and juice of 2 oranges
2 cinnamon sticks
½ teaspoon grated fresh nutmeg
3 cloves
300 ml water
1 x 750 ml bottle red wine
1 red apple, cored and thickly sliced
1 extra orange, sliced

Serves 6–8

Put the sugar, orange rind and juice, cinnamon, nutmeg and cloves into a large saucepan. Add water and bring to the boil. Simmer for 10–15 minutes then add the wine, apple and orange slices. Bring to a simmer and serve, not too hot, in heatproof glasses.

For a non-alcoholic drink, substitute grape, apple or cranberry juice or a fruity herbal tea for the wine.

Smoked Salmon Savouries

Other smoked fish such as trout could easily be substituted for the salmon in this recipe.

24 slices fresh white
  sandwich-cut bread
butter for spreading
250 g crème fraîche or
  sour cream

200 g hot-smoked salmon or sliced
  smoked salmon in a piece
50 g salmon caviar
freshly ground black pepper
sprigs of parsley to garnish

Makes 24

Preheat oven to 180°C.

Remove the crusts from the bread slices, then flatten each slice with a rolling pin. Press out circles of bread with a 5–6 cm cookie cutter. Butter one side. Carefully press, buttered side down, into mini muffin tins. Bake for 15–18 minutes until crisp and golden brown. Cool on a wire rack.

To serve, place 1 teaspoon of crème fraîche in each case and top with a twist of sliced smoked salmon and ½ teaspoon of salmon caviar. Garnish with a grind of pepper and a tiny sprig of parsley.

Pimm's Cocktails

Perfect for a summer's day after tennis, or 5 o'clock drinks.

crushed ice
200 ml Pimm's
slices of seasonal fresh fruit (orange, apples,
  cucumber, fresh berries etc)
mint sprigs
dry ginger ale and/or lemonade

Serves 4

Fill two thirds of a 1.5 litre jug with ice and pour in the Pimm's. Add some fresh fruit and a generous handful of mint sprigs. Top with dry ginger ale or lemonade, or a mix of both. Serve in tall glasses.

Pistachio Morsels

100 g butter, chilled and cubed
100 g tasty cheese, grated (approximately 1 cup grated)
1 cup flour
½ teaspoon salt
100 g mozzarella cheese, cut into 36 little cubes
36 pistachio nuts, shelled

Makes 36

Preheat oven to 180°C. Spray little silicon moulds or mini muffin tins with non-stick baking spray.

Place the chilled butter cubes, grated cheese, flour and salt into a food processor and mix well until formed into a clump of pastry around the blade. Roll into 36 small balls and place into the prepared tins. Press a tiny cube of mozzarella and a pistachio nut into each ball of pastry and bake for approximately 15 minutes, until the pastry is golden and the mozzarella toasty and melted. Cool in the tin then twist the tin to remove. Serve warm.

Spiced Roast Macadamias

1 teaspoon cumin seeds
1 teaspoon coriander seeds
1 tablespoon sesame seeds
2 cups shelled macadamia nuts
1 egg white, lightly whisked until foamy
2 teaspoons salt

Makes 2 cups

Preheat oven to 180°C.

Sprinkle the cumin, coriander and sesame seeds in a roasting dish and bake for about 10–12 minutes until the seeds are toasted golden and fragrant. Whiz the seeds in a spice or coffee grinder, or crush with a mortar and pestle. Toss the ground seeds, macadamias, egg white and salt together in a bowl until each nut is well coated. Spread out in the roasting dish and bake for about 12 minutes, until the nuts are golden and crisp. Cool completely and store in an airtight container.

Warm Spinach and Artichoke Dip

1 x 400 g can artichoke hearts in brine or water
1 cup mayonnaise (whole-egg mayonnaise
  such as Best brand)
1 cup grated Parmesan cheese
1½ cups grated tasty cheese
350 g frozen spinach, thawed
1 teaspoon Worcestershire sauce
salt and freshly ground black pepper

Serves 6

Preheat oven to 160°C. Spray a 20 cm lasagne or quiche dish with non-stick baking spray.

Drain the artichoke hearts and chop each one into about 6 pieces. Mix these with the mayonnaise and grated cheeses. Press the spinach down firmly in a sieve to extract as much liquid as possible, then mix the drained spinach into the cheese and artichoke mixture. Stir in the Worcestershire sauce and season with salt and pepper.

Spread in the prepared dish and bake for 20 minutes until the surface is browning and the mixture bubbly. Serve warm with crostini. I usually place this dip in the container on a board surrounded by crostini and with a couple of pâté knives to spread.

Broad Bean Guacamole with Turkish Bread Crostini

Adding the word 'guacamole' really helped with the naming of this dish. When I called it broad bean purée, no one was game to try it, but a dash of poetic licence and a little name substitution have had everyone coming back for second and third dips.

3 cups broad beans (approximately) — can be frozen
5 cloves garlic, roasted or microwaved
3 tablespoons extra virgin olive oil
grated rind and juice of 1 lemon
salt and freshly ground black pepper
1 loaf Turkish bread
½ cup extra olive oil (approximately)
garlic salt to sprinkle

Serves 8

Preheat oven to 200°C.

Cook the beans in boiling water for 5 minutes. Rinse in cool water and peel. This is easy to do, using your fingernail to split the grey skins and popping out the tender green inners. Purée the beans, cooked garlic, oil, lemon rind and juice and salt and pepper, until a smooth paste forms. Taste to check you've seasoned well. It needs to taste of plenty of lemon and pepper. Store covered in the fridge before serving.

Slice the Turkish bread into approximately 36 thin slices, brush generously with olive oil and sprinkle with garlic salt. Roast in a hot oven for 8–10 minutes until crispy and golden brown. Once the crostini have cooled on a wire rack, they can be stored in an airtight container.

Pesto Cheese Puffs

2 sheets flaky pastry
1 small tub (approximately ½ cup) basil pine nut pesto
1 cup grated tasty cheese
1 small bunch parsley, broken into little sprigs
3 eggs
1 cup cream
salt and freshly ground black pepper

Makes 36

Preheat oven to 180°C. Spray mini muffin tins or tiny tart tins with non-stick baking spray.

Using a 4–5 cm round cookie cutter, stamp out circles of pastry and press into prepared tins. Divide the pesto, grated cheese and sprigs of parsley between the pastry cases. Mix in the eggs and cream and season with salt and pepper. Pour a little (about 1–2 teaspoons) into each case.

Bake for 20–25 minutes until puffed and golden. These puff up then deflate as they cool. Serve warm or reheated.

Baby Frittatas

1 small courgette, finely diced
1 small red pepper, deseeded and
  finely diced
3 slices shaved ham,
  chopped finely
6 eggs
2 tablespoons cream
2 tablespoons corn flour

1 tablespoon chopped chives
1 tablespoon chopped parsley
1 teaspoon lemon pepper seasoning
½ cup finely chopped feta
½ cup finely grated Parmesan cheese
tiny sprigs of fresh marjoram,
  thyme or parsley to garnish

Makes 24

Preheat oven to 180°C. Spray 2 trays of mini muffin tins with non-stick baking spray.

Mix all the ingredients together in a blender and process in short bursts to combine. Pour into the tins till three-quarters full. Cook for 10–15 minutes until puffed and set. Serve immediately, garnished with tiny sprigs of fresh marjoram, thyme or parsley.

Baby Frittatas

Sticky Cocktail Sausages

An all-time favourite nibble for drinks parties.

1 kg cocktail sausages (or small chipolata sausages)
3 tablespoons liquid honey or maple syrup
6 tablespoons hoisin sauce
1 teaspoon mustard seeds or sesame seeds

Serves 10–12

Preheat oven to 180°C.

Place sausages in a large bowl or ziplock plastic bag. Add the honey, hoisin sauce and seeds and squish around to evenly coat the sausages.

Place the sausages in a roasting tin and roast for about 40 minutes, stirring a couple of times until golden brown and cooked through. Serve warm with toothpicks, cocktail forks or bamboo skewers as the sausages are quite sticky to handle. These are just delicious and you can never seem to cook enough.

A handy tip — if you can't find baby cocktail sausages, use chipolatas and just twist each one into 2–3 small sausages. Cook before cutting them into individual sausages.

How to cook perfect sausages

Do not prick them before cooking as their flavour and juices will escape, making the sausages dry. The skins are also more likely to split if they have been pricked.

Fry in just a dash of oil in a non-stick frypan over a medium heat for 20 minutes, turning now and again, until golden brown. Alternatively bake, brushed with oil, in a roasting tin with the oven at 180°C and set to fan bake. Cook for 25 minutes, tossing occasionally.

A grace :
Bless, O Lord, before we dine
Each dish of food, each cup of wine
And bless our hearts, that we may be
Aware of what we owe to thee

Asian Chicken and Coriander Bites

These bites are perfect to have with drinks.

> 500 g minced chicken
> ½ cup hoisin sauce
> 2 teaspoons Asian fish sauce
> 1 long red chilli, deseeded and finely chopped
> 3 tablespoons chopped coriander or parsley
> 2–3 cloves garlic, crushed (about 1 teaspoon)

Makes 36

Preheat oven to 200°C. Spray three 12-cup mini muffin tins with non-stick baking spray. Place all ingredients in a food processor and whiz to blend well. Divide the mixture between the prepared tins (approximately 1 teaspoon per muffin cup).

Bake for 15 minutes. Serve warm with toothpicks and sweet chilli sauce for dipping.

Gin-soaked Apricots Wrapped in Bacon

> ½ cup gin – Seagers, of course!
> 30 dried apricots (Otago apricots
>   have the best flavour)
> 10 rashers rindless streaky bacon

Makes 30

Place the dried apricots in a microwave-proof bowl and pour the gin over them. Add a little more gin or some water if necessary, so they are all just covered by the liquid. Microwave on high for 2–3 minutes and stir, then microwave for a couple more minutes. Leave apricots to soak up all the gin and to plump up and cool. Preheat the oven to 200°C.

Cut each bacon rasher into 3 strips. Wrap a strip of bacon around each apricot and secure with a toothpick. Bake for approximately 10–12 minutes, until the bacon is crisp and golden. Secure with fresh toothpicks or decorative cocktail sticks before serving.

5

THE MAIN EVENT, SIDE DISHES & SALADS

Tarragon Chicken Pie

1 tablespoon oil

1 tablespoon butter

3 spring onions, finely sliced

3 medium onions, peeled and
  chopped

5 rashers rindless bacon, chopped

4 chicken breasts, skinless, boneless
  and cut into fingers

salt and freshly ground black pepper

1 cup chicken stock

1 cup frozen baby peas

6 sprigs tarragon, chopped

3 slices shaved ham, rolled up
  and cut into ribbons

50 ml cream

2 sheets frozen puff pastry, thawed

1 egg yolk and 1 tablespoon
  water to glaze

Serves 4

In a large frypan heat the oil and butter. Add the spring onion, onion and bacon.
Cook for 3–4 minutes. Add the chicken, season with salt and pepper and stir-
fry a couple of minutes. Pour in the stock, peas and tarragon. Simmer for 8–10
minutes, then add the ham and cream. Cool.

   Spray a medium-sized pie plate with non-stick baking spray. Tip the chicken
mixture into the prepared pie dish. Brush one sheet of pastry with water then
press on the other sheet. Roll together then cut out and cover the pie. Cut holes
to allow steam to escape and chill the whole dish for at least an hour.

Preheat oven to 200°C.
Mix the egg yolk with the
water and brush over pastry.
Bake for 25–30 minutes until
pastry is puffed and golden and
the filling heated through.

Horseradish and Lemon-crusted Salmon

A great recipe for serving salmon to a crowd without pan-frying.

1 tablespoon prepared
   horseradish sauce
½ cup chopped parsley
grated rind and juice of
   2 lemons
½ teaspoon lemon pepper
   seasoning
1 egg white

salt and freshly ground
   black pepper
1 cup panko (Japanese
   breadcrumbs)
2 tablespoons lite olive oil
6 portions salmon, skin on or off as
   desired, all visible bones removed
hollandaise sauce to serve

Serves 6

Preheat oven to 220°C. Line a roasting dish with a sheet of non-stick baking paper.

   Mix the horseradish, parsley, lemon rind and juice, lemon pepper seasoning, egg white, salt and pepper, panko and oil together with a fork. Just mix loosely; don't be too vigorous combining them.

   Place the salmon portions, skin side down, in the prepared roasting dish. Divide the crumb mixture evenly over the salmon and gently press it onto each piece. Bake for 12–15 minutes until the fish is just cooked through and the crumbs are a nice, toasty golden. Serve with hollandaise sauce and some healthy vegetables or a salad.

Honey Mustard Fish Fillets

1 tablespoon clear honey
1 tablespoon wholegrain mustard
2 tablespoons light soy sauce
grated rind and juice of 1 lime

3 tablespoons white wine
   or water
4 boneless fresh fish fillets
4 spring onions, sliced

Serves 4

Mix the honey, mustard, soy sauce, lime rind and juice and wine together.

   Heat a large non-stick pan and cook the fish fillets. (I don't use any oil for this.) Cook for 2–3 minutes, depending on the thickness of the fillets, then carefully turn over. Pour sauce over the top and bring to the boil. Sprinkle the sliced spring onions on top and serve. This is great with rice and a salad.

Horseradish and Lemon-crusted Salmon

Spinach and Mozzarella Chicken in Tomato Sauce

FOR THE TOMATO SAUCE
1 tablespoon olive oil
1 onion, chopped
2 garlic cloves, crushed
400 g can chopped tomatoes
5-6 fresh basil leaves,
  chopped
salt and freshly ground black pepper

FOR THE CHICKEN
2 tablespoons oil
4 chicken breasts, boneless and
  skinless
salt and freshly ground
  black pepper
3 handfuls baby spinach leaves
¼ cup grated mozzarella cheese

Serves 4

Preheat oven to 190°C.

For the sauce, heat the oil in a saucepan and gently fry the onion and garlic until softened. Stir in the tomatoes, basil, salt and pepper. Cook, covered, for about 20 minutes until thickened.

Heat the oil in a pan and quickly brown the chicken all over. Season with salt and pepper. Microwave the spinach for 1 minute to wilt.

Place the wilted spinach in an ovenproof dish, then put the chicken on top. Pour tomato sauce over the top and sprinkle with grated mozzarella. Cook for about 25 minutes until the chicken is cooked through and the mozzarella has melted. Serve piping hot.

Garlic Parmesan Crumbed Chicken Breasts

6 chicken breasts, boneless and skinless
½ cup thick American-style mayonnaise
¼ cup grated Parmesan cheese

1 teaspoon garlic salt
4 slices toast-cut bread, crusts removed
1 tablespoon chopped parsley

Serves 6

Preheat oven to 200°C.

Place the chicken breasts in an ovenproof dish (such as a small lasagne dish). Spread the mayonnaise over the chicken, like buttering toast. Place the Parmesan, garlic salt, bread slices and parsley in a food processor and whizz to produce a coarse crumb texture. Sprinkle over the chicken, pressing down to help it stick. Bake for 20–25 minutes until the chicken is cooked through and the crumbs are toasty and golden brown. Serve with seasonal vegetables or a salad.

Spinach and Mozzarella Chicken in Tomato Sauce

Fisherman's Pies

A real 'home is the sailor, home from the sea' dish: the fisherman's version of shepherd's pie.

FOR THE POTATO TOPPING
1 kg potatoes suitable for mashing
generous knob of butter or margarine
½ cup sour cream or crème fraîche
salt and freshly ground black pepper

FOR THE FILLING
1 small onion, peeled and
    roughly chopped
500 ml milk
1 x 500 g can smoked fish fillets in brine
250 g smoked salmon trimmings

2 cups chopped white boneless fish fillets
1 cup prawns or shrimps
½ cup chopped gherkins
3 hard-boiled eggs, cut into wedges
3 tablespoons chopped parsley
grated rind and juice of 1 lemon
1 cup thawed baby peas
50 g butter
3 tablespoons flour
50 ml cream or milk
freshly ground black pepper
½ cup grated tasty cheese

Serves 6

Peel the potatoes and cook until tender, approximately 20 minutes. Put them through a potato ricer or mash until fluffy and lump free. Beat in the butter and sour cream and season with salt and pepper.

Place the onion and milk in a small saucepan and bring to the boil, then cool, allowing the onion to infuse into the milk. Strain when cool and discard the onion.

Place all the fish and prawns in a bowl, draining but reserving the liquid from the canned smoked fish fillets. Add the gherkins, egg, parsley, lemon juice and rind and peas.

Melt the butter over a low heat and add the flour, whisking to combine. Cook for about 1 minute then whisk in the milk and reserved fish liquid, a little bit at a time. Keep stirring as it thickens. Add the cream and pepper. There's no need for extra salt as the smoked fish is quite salty. Pour sauce over the fish, gently stirring through to combine, being careful not to over-mix and break up the chunks of fish.

Spray 6 small noodle bowls or ramekins with non-stick baking spray. Divide the mixture between them, then spread the mashed potato over and sprinkle with grated cheese. Bake for 35–40 minutes until piping hot with the top golden and crispy.

Baby Beef Wellingtons

These individual portions of fillet steak are topped with garlic cream cheese and wrapped in puff pastry parcels.

4 x 100 g fillet steaks
salt and freshly ground black pepper
2 sheets frozen puff pastry, thawed
150 g garlic and herb-flavoured cream cheese
1 egg yolk, beaten with 1 teaspoon of
  cold water, to glaze

Serves 4

Sprinkle the steaks with salt and pepper and sear quickly in a hot pan or on a grill plate. Cook for only 1 minute maximum each side. Cool the steaks.

Cut the pastry sheets in half and cut a thin strip of pastry off each sheet so that you have 4 ribbons, each 3 mm wide. Divide the cheese into four and spread on each cooled steak. Wrap the steaks in pastry, cheese side down, to form small parcels. Wet the edges to secure. Turn the parcels cheese-side up and decorate each with a pastry ribbon, sticking it down with water.

Brush the pastry all over with the beaten egg yolk and place on a baking tray, seam-side down. Chill for 20 minutes while you preheat oven to 200°C. Cook for approximately 25 minutes, until the pastry is golden and the steak medium rare.

These can be prepared ahead and frozen for up to a month. They can be cooked from frozen, but will take approximately 35–40 minutes.

Farmhouse-style Corned Beef with Mustard Sauce

I like to cook corned beef in a crockpot or in the Aga. This long, slow method was the norm in the 'olden days' but of course it can be done much more quickly in a covered saucepan, keeping an eye on the liquid level, topping up as necessary and gently boiling for 1½ –2 hours.

FOR THE BEEF
1.5 kg piece (approximately) corned silverside
2 onions, peeled and roughly chopped
10 whole peppercorns
2 bay leaves (3 if using fresh bay leaves)
2 heaped tablespoons dark cane sugar

FOR THE MUSTARD SAUCE
1 cup of the corned beef stock
*   (the liquid it's been cooked in)*
½ cup malt vinegar
2 eggs
¼ cup sugar
2 teaspoons dried mustard powder
1 tablespoon flour

Serves 4–6
Place the beef and other cooking ingredients in a crockpot and cover with water. Cover and cook on low for 8–10 hours.

To make the sauce, whisk all the ingredients together and gently heat in a small saucepan, stirring continuously with a wire whisk as the sauce cooks and thickens. Remove from the heat just as it comes to the boil.

Serve sauce warm with generous slices of corned beef. Traditional accompaniments are boiled spuddies, carrot and cabbage. The mustard sauce is wonderful cold as a mayonnaise-type dressing on a corned beef sandwich, and my family likes it stirred through pasta with leftover corned beef shredded up finely and lots of fresh parsley.

The great gift of appetite is that there is always something new and fresh to savour.

Winter's Night Venison Casserole

1.5 kg venison, cut into 4 cm cubes
2 teaspoons freshly ground black pepper
8 juniper berries, crushed or
   ground like peppercorns
1 tablespoon fresh thyme leaves
2 medium onions, peeled and chopped
300 ml red wine
100 ml olive oil
4 tablespoons canola or lite olive oil
8 rashers rindless streaky bacon, chopped
2–3 cloves garlic, crushed (about 1 teaspoon)

2 tablespoons flour
300 ml venison or beef stock
2 bay leaves
salt
25 g butter
1 teaspoon honey
225 g vacuum-packed or
   tinned chestnuts (optional)
1 cup craisins (dried
   cranberries)
1 cup chopped pitted prunes

Serves 6

Place the meat in a large bowl with the pepper, juniper berries, thyme, onion, red wine and olive oil. Mix together, cover and marinate for 24 hours.

Remove the venison and reserve the marinade. Pat the meat dry with paper towels. Heat 4 tablespoons of oil in a flameproof casserole, preferably cast iron, and brown the chunks of venison in batches over high heat. Remove them as they brown. Add the bacon to the casserole and sizzle for 4–5 minutes to brown, then add the garlic. Lower the heat and stir in the flour, mixing well. Add the reserved marinade and bring to the boil. Return the meat to the casserole and add the stock and bay leaves. Season with salt. Cover and place in the oven, set to 160°C. Cook for 2 hours.

In a non-stick frypan, melt the butter and honey. Add the chestnuts, cranberries and prunes. Mix well to coat in the honey butter, then stir this whole pan-load into the casserole. Return the casserole to the oven for 15–20 minutes then serve.

Paprika Baked Potatoes

4 medium-sized potatoes
olive oil spray

salt to sprinkle
smoked paprika (about 1 teaspoon)

Serves 4

Preheat oven to 200°C. Scrub the potatoes, then slice them in half lengthways. Using the tip of a small vegetable knife, score lines across the cut surface. Place cut-side up in a roasting dish. Spray (or brush) with olive oil then sprinkle with salt and paprika. Bake for approximately 45 minutes.

Parmesan Yorkshires

½ cup flour
½ teaspoon salt
1 large egg

75 ml water
75 ml milk
¼ cup grated Parmesan cheese

Makes 12 muffin-sized Yorkshires, or 36 small ones

Preheat oven to 220°C. Spray muffin tins generously with non-stick baking spray and place in the oven to heat for 5 minutes.

Place all ingredients in a blender and mix until creamy and smooth.

Fill the muffin tins three-quarters full with mixture and bake for 15–20 minutes (10–12 minutes for mini muffin size) until golden brown and puffed up. They can be cooked in advance then quickly returned to the oven to reheat before serving. These are perfect to serve with classic roast beef, but are also great with everyday sausages.

Roast Lamb with Coffee and Cream

I know this seems very strange, but believe me it is truly delicious. No one who eats it can ever guess what the secret ingredients are!

1 leg of lamb (approximately 2.5 kg)
3 large onions, roughly quartered
 (no need to peel)
300 ml hot, strong, unsweetened
 black espresso coffee
2 tablespoons flour

25 g butter
2 cups hot lamb or beef stock
 (can be made from cubes)
3 tablespoons redcurrant jelly
½ cup crème fraîche
salt and freshly ground black pepper

Serves 6

Preheat oven to 220°C.

Place the leg of lamb and the onion quarters into a roasting dish and cook for 45 minutes. Turn the temperature down to 180°C, pour the hot coffee over the meat and continue roasting for a further hour, or until the lamb is cooked to your liking. Remove the meat from the roasting dish and keep warm, covered in a tinfoil tent.

Strain off the liquid from the roasting tin and reserve, discarding the onion. Sprinkle the flour into the tin, add the butter and whisk together. Gradually whisk in the strained coffee liquid and the hot lamb stock. Cook for 3–4 minutes, stirring as it thickens like a gravy. Stir in the redcurrant jelly and crème fraîche and season to taste with salt and pepper. Serve the lamb with the sauce poured over as a gravy.

Parmesan Yorkshires

Family Favourite Lemon Fish

1 tablespoon oil
50 g butter
4 medium-sized fresh fish fillets (any
   sort of white fish can be used), sliced
   thinly into pencil-sized strips
juice and grated rind of two juicy lemons

½ cup chopped Italian
   parsley
2 cups cherry tomato halves
2 cups cooked rice
salt and freshly ground black
   pepper

Serves 4

In a large non-stick frypan, heat the oil and butter until sizzling. Toss in the fish, lemon juice and rind. Stir-fry for 1–2 minutes only, until the fish just turns opaque. Add parsley, tomatoes and rice. Stir to heat through. Season with salt and pepper, then serve immediately. This dish is great with tiny new potatoes and salad.

Smoked Snapper Kedgeree

1 kg smoked snapper fillets, or
   other smoked fish
125 g butter
1 tablespoon oil
1 onion, chopped
1 cup long-grain or basmati rice

1 tablespoon mild curry paste or
   2 teaspoons curry powder
1 cup frozen peas
3 tablespoons drained capers
3 hard-boiled eggs, chopped
2 tablespoons chopped parsley

Serves 4–6

Place the smoked fish in a deep bowl and cover with 700 ml of boiling water. Leave to sit for 10 minutes, then drain but reserve the soaking water. Skin and flake the fish, removing any bones, then set aside.

Heat half the butter and all the oil in a large pan. Add the onion and cook over medium heat for 3–4 minutes. Add the rice and curry paste. Stir for 2 minutes, pour in the reserved soaking liquid, bring to the boil then reduce heat so it just simmers. Cover the pan and leave to cook for 8–9 minutes. Stir in the peas, capers and fish. Cover again and cook for 5 minutes until all the liquid is absorbed (add a wee bit of water if it's still too dry).

Remove from heat and dot over the remaining butter, stirring it in, then garnish with the chopped egg and parsley. Great served with mango chutney and, if desired, lemon wedges to squeeze over.

Family Favourite Lemon Fish

Shearers' Browned Onion Meat Pies

1 tablespoon cornflour

3 tablespoons tomato sauce

2 tablespoons Worcestershire sauce

1 teaspoon Marmite or Vegemite

½ cup boiling water

½ teaspoon each salt and
   freshly ground black pepper

2 tablespoons oil

2 medium onions, peeled
   and finely chopped

1–2 cloves garlic, crushed
   (about ½ teaspoon)

500 g lean beef mince

2 sheets frozen shortcrust
   pastry

2 sheets frozen puff pastry

1 teaspoon cold water,
   to seal

1 egg yolk, beaten,
   to glaze

Makes 4

Combine the cornflour, tomato sauce, Worcestershire sauce, Marmite, boiling water and salt and pepper. Stir until the Marmite has dissolved. Set aside.

Heat the oil in a frypan and add the onion and garlic. Cook for 5 minutes, stirring over a medium to high heat to brown the onion. Add the mince and stir-fry until browned. Reduce heat to a simmer and stir in the liquid. Keep stirring until the mixture thickens. Cool completely.

Preheat oven to 200°C. Spray 4 large cup-sized pie tins with non-stick baking spray. Cut 2 circles of shortcrust pastry from each sheet. Line the tins with these. Spoon in the cooled mince mixture, brush the pastry edges with cold water and cover with circles of puff pastry, pressing the edges together with a fork to seal. Brush the tops with beaten egg yolk and bake for 30–35 minutes until the pastry is puffed and golden. Leave in the tins for 5 minutes before turning out to serve.

Lamb Cutlets with Fresh Mint and Sweet Chilli Chutney

FRESH MINT AND SWEET CHILLI CHUTNEY
2 big handfuls mint leaves, washed
*   and shaken dry*
3 onions, peeled and quartered
3 apples, cored, skin on
1 large cup raisins
500 ml cider vinegar
2 cups sugar
2 teaspoons salt
1 teaspoon mustard powder
½ cup sweet chilli sauce
1 tablespoon chopped fresh mint,
*   to serve*

24–36 lamb cutlets (4–6 lamb
*   cutlets per serving)*
2 tablespoons oil
1 tablespoon Worcestershire sauce
1 teaspoon garlic salt
freshly ground black pepper
fresh mint sprigs to garnish

Serves 6

To make the chutney, place the mint leaves, onions, apples and raisins in a food processor and finely chop into a pulp. Tip into a large saucepan. Add the vinegar, sugar, salt and mustard. Bring to the boil, then gently boil for 30 minutes until thick and chutney-like. Cool and stir in the sweet chilli sauce. Store in the fridge. Just before serving, stir through a tablespoon of chopped mint.

To cook the lamb, preheat oven to 200°C.

Using a meat mallet, give each cutlet a good whack to flatten the meaty portion. Heat the oil in a large non-stick ovenproof pan and sear the cutlets for 2–3 minutes. Turn over and sprinkle the cooked side with Worcestershire sauce, garlic salt and pepper. Sear second side (about 1 minute). Remove and set aside while you cook the remaining cutlets. Return to the pan and place in the preheated oven for 10 minutes. Serve with a good dollop of chutney and garnish with mint sprigs. The cutlets can be tossed with blanched green beans and strawberries.

Lamb cooking guide

The time a joint of meat takes to cook properly depends solely on its weight.

My tried and tested method for lamb is to preheat the oven to 180°C; turn the setting to fan bake, if you have it. Roast the joint for 25 minutes per 450 g, plus 25 minutes more. This is for pink but not bloody meat. For slightly more well-done meat, with a little pinkness showing but still very tender, increase cooking time to 30 minutes per 450 g, plus 30 minutes more.

Remove meat to a plate and cover with tinfoil made into a tent. Rest it for 15 minutes before carving. Any juices that run out of the joint can be added to the gravy.

A boned shoulder of lamb is my personal favourite — no bones and all meat, so easy-peasy to carve up. Allow 150–200 g per person.

I don't think friends come to dinner with their clipboards ready to mark you out of ten — have a little faith in yourself. Cooking with passion and the desire to please someone is what really makes all the difference.

Schnitzels with Noodles and Anchovy Caper Dressing

This is an easy-to-prepare meal but it is always impressive for dinner parties and doesn't cost the earth. Any crumbed schnitzel can be used — pork, chicken or beef.

1 packet (500 g) fresh ribbon noodles or
fettuccini-style pasta
2 tablespoons butter, or olive oil or margarine
2 tablespoons fresh lemon juice
2–3 tablespoons oil for frying
6 portions crumbed schnitzel
12 anchovy fillets, coarsely chopped
¼ cup drained capers, chopped
¼ cup chopped parsley
lemon wedges, to serve
250 g lite sour cream

Serves 6

Bring a large saucepan of salted water to the boil and cook the noodles according to packet instructions — about 5 minutes — then drain and toss with the butter and lemon juice.

Meanwhile, heat a large, preferably non-stick, frypan with 1–2 tablespoons of the oil. Pan-fry the schnitzels until golden brown, adding a little extra oil as required. Drain on paper towels.

Mix the anchovies, capers and parsley together and set aside.

To serve, place the noodles on a platter, lie the schnitzels on top and sprinkle over the anchovy-caper mixture. Garnish with lemon wedges. Pass a bowl of sour cream around for people to serve themselves.

Chinese Restaurant-style Sticky Lemon Chicken

8 chicken breasts, skinless and boneless
½ cup corn flour
4 egg yolks
4 tablespoons water
salt and freshly ground black pepper
oil for frying
5 spring onions, finely sliced,
   to garnish

FOR THE LEMON SAUCE
grated rind and juice of 3 lemons
2 teaspoons chicken stock powder
2 tablespoons cornflour
2 tablespoons honey
3 tablespoons brown sugar
1 teaspoon grated fresh ginger
1¾ cups water

Serves 6

Pound the chicken breasts between sheets of cling film or baking paper until flattened like schnitzels. Whisk the cornflour, egg yolks and water together, adding the salt and pepper. Dip the chicken breasts, cutting in half if necessary, into the batter, shaking off the excess. Cook a few at a time in oil, in a deep fryer, until golden brown. Keep these warm while you cook the remaining chicken.

For the sauce, mix all the ingredients together in a saucepan, stirring over medium heat. As the mixture comes to the boil it should thicken and clear.

Arrange on a serving plate, spoon sauce over it and sprinkle with spring onion. Serve with crisp green salad and rice.

Coconut Chicken Curry

1 tablespoon sesame oil
2 tablespoons green curry paste
4 chicken breasts, skinless and boneless,
   cut into fingers
1 cup coconut cream

1 tablespoon Asian fish sauce
5 spring onions, sliced
salt and freshly ground black
   pepper
½ cup chopped coriander

Serves 4

Heat the oil in a non-stick frypan or wok and cook the curry paste for 30 seconds. Add the chicken strips and stir-fry for 5–6 minutes, until cooked through. Add the coconut cream and fish sauce, and cook for 3–4 more minutes. Add the spring onions. Check the seasoning, adding salt and pepper to taste. Garnish with chopped coriander and serve with rice.

Chinese Restaurant-style Sticky Lemon Chicken

Anyone who is interested in cooking is interested in knowing more.

Maple-glazed Meatloaf

FOR THE MEATLOAF
1 celery stalk, finely chopped
2 carrots, peeled and chopped
1 medium-sized onion, peeled and
    finely chopped
2–3 cloves garlic, crushed
    (about 1 teaspoon)
2 teaspoons dried thyme
1 teaspoon dried mustard powder
1 tablespoon grainy mustard
1 egg

1 cup fresh breadcrumbs,
    made in a food processor
750 g mince (a mixture of pork and
    beef is good)
4 tablespoons tomato sauce or ketchup
salt and freshly ground black pepper

FOR THE GLAZE
½ cup pure maple syrup
3 tablespoons tomato sauce or
    ketchup

Serves 6

Preheat oven to 200°C. Line a 20 x 30 cm spring-roll tin with tinfoil.

Mix all meatloaf ingredients together by hand, wearing disposable gloves. Form into a log shape and lift into the prepared tin.

Combine the glaze ingredients and brush half the mixture over the meatloaf. Cook for 30 minutes, then brush with the rest of the mixture and cook a further 15–20 minutes until golden brown and cooked through. Serve sliced with mashed potato, creamy polenta and seasonal vegetables or salad.

Roast Potatoes with Crispy Polenta Crusts

6-8 large roasting potatoes
3 tablespoons olive oil

½ cup fine cornmeal or polenta
sea salt flakes

Serves 6

Preheat oven to 200°C. Peel and cut the potatoes into evenly sized pieces. Place in a pot of cold salted water, cover, and bring to the boil. Boil for 10 minutes. Drain and shake the potatoes about in the saucepan to roughen up and crush the edges. Sprinkle the cornmeal over and shake to coat evenly.

Heat the oil in a roasting dish until very hot before adding the potatoes. Turn to coat well in the oil and roast about 45 minutes, stirring a couple of times, until the potatoes are golden and crispy. Sprinkle with sea salt flakes before serving. Make sure the potatoes are served piping hot to maintain crispness.

To oven-roast garlic

Slice whole bulbs of fresh garlic through the centre.
Drizzle with extra virgin olive oil and sea salt. Bake at
180°C for 30–35 minutes until soft and very fragrant.

Moroccan-spiced Cauliflower with Mint

1 medium-sized cauliflower,
    divided into florets
3 tablespoons olive oil
1 teaspoon paprika
½ teaspoon ground cumin

½ teaspoon ground coriander
½ teaspoon turmeric
salt and freshly ground black pepper
½ cup roughly chopped fresh mint
    leaves

Serves 4–6

Steam or boil the cauliflower until just tender. Don't overcook or it will turn to mush. Drain and allow to cool and dry off a little.

Heat the oil in a saucepan (I use the same saucepan I've cooked the cauli in). When this is sizzling, add the spices and salt and pepper. Cook for 30 seconds, then add the cauliflower and toss to coat well. Check the seasoning and sprinkle with the fresh mint. Serve chilled or at room temperature.

Asian-style Salad

I like this salad as it can be all prepared in advance with no wilting salad leaves. It is great in winter when lettuces are scarce and expensive.

FOR THE DRESSING
2 tablespoons Asian fish sauce
juice and grated rind of 2 limes
3 tablespoons sweet chilli sauce
1 tablespoon sesame oil
3 tablespoons olive oil

FOR THE SALAD
2 cups (1 punnet) cherry tomatoes,
    halved

2 cups diced telegraph cucumber
1 cup finely sliced celery
2 spring onions, finely sliced
4 cups finely shredded
    Chinese cabbage (or
    savoy cabbage)
½ cup chopped parsley
2 tablespoons chopped
    coriander

Serves 4–6

Make the dressing by mixing all the ingredients in a large salad bowl, using a wire whisk to combine. Add the salad ingredients to the bowl and toss to spread the dressing. Serve immediately in individual noodle bowls.

Moroccan-spiced Cauliflower with Mint

Colcannon Jacket Potatoes

4 medium to large potatoes,
  scrubbed but not peeled
2 tablespoons oil
3 rashers lean bacon, chopped
1 onion, peeled and finely
  chopped

2 cups finely shredded cabbage
  (crinkly savoy or Chinese
  cabbage is best)
3 tablespoons chopped parsley
salt and freshly ground black pepper
½ cup grated tasty cheese

Serves 4

Bake the potatoes in a 200°C oven for 30–40 minutes until cooked, or microwave to speed up the process. Once cool enough to handle, cut off and set aside the tops. Scoop the cooked potato into a bowl and mash with a fork.

Heat the oil in a large frypan. Add the chopped bacon and onion and cook for 3 minutes before adding the cabbage. Stir-fry for a few minutes. Add the mashed potato and parsley, and season with salt and pepper. Spoon the mixture back into the potato jackets, sprinkle with grated cheese and replace the 'lids'.

These can be prepared up to a day in advance and stored in the fridge. Reheat either in the oven or the microwave to serve.

Root Vegetable Gratin

A wonderful side dish or simply a winter's meal on its own.

500 g each carrots, parsnips,
  swede and kumara
1 cup crème fraîche
½ cup milk

1 tablespoon prepared horseradish
  sauce
salt and freshly ground black pepper
1 cup grated tasty cheese

Serves 6

Preheat oven to 200°C. Spray a large gratin or lasagne dish with non-stick baking spray. Peel and chop the vegetables to evenly sized smallish pieces. Bring a large saucepan of salted water to the boil. Toss in the carrots for 5 minutes, then add the parsnips, swede and kumara. Cook a further 6–8 minutes until the vegetable pieces are tender when pierced with a fork. Drain and tip the vegetables into the prepared dish. Mix the crème fraîche, milk and horseradish together, and season with salt and pepper. Spread this over the vegetables and sprinkle the grated cheese over the top. Bake for approximately 30 minutes until golden brown and crispy on top.

Colcannon Jacket Potatoes

Barbecued Stuffed Peppers

3 large peppers (red, green or yellow —
  or a combination)
2 cups halved or quartered cherry tomatoes
150 g feta cheese, cut into small cubes

½ cup grated tasty cheese
1 cup coarsely chopped parsley
freshly ground black pepper and
  a little salt

Serves 6

Cut the peppers in half vertically and scoop out the seeds. Mix together the cherry tomatoes, feta, grated tasty cheese, parsley and a generous amount of black pepper (a little salt may also be added, depending on the saltiness of the feta), and spoon into the half pepper shells. Cook on a preheated BBQ grill for 15–20 minutes. I find closing the lid of the BBQ a good idea as it cooks them more quickly and melts the cheese filling. Serve immediately. Overcooking will make them too mushy and soft and therefore hard to serve.

Oven-baked Chicken Risotto

Terribly easy risotto that's creamy and drop-dead impressive — guests will think you've been hand-stirring it for hours.

50 g butter
1 large onion, peeled and finely chopped
2 chicken breasts, boneless, skinless and
  cut into small strips
2 cups arborio rice
½ cup white wine

5 cups well-flavoured chicken stock
  (can be made from powder or cubes)
2 cups sliced button mushrooms
2 cups grated Parmesan cheese
½ cup sliced marinated roast peppers
2 tablespoons chopped Italian parsley

Serves 4

Preheat oven to 170°C. Place a medium-sized lasagne dish or casserole into the oven to heat.

Melt the butter in a saucepan. Add the onion and cook for 2 minutes. Add the chicken and rice and cook a further 2 minutes, stirring. Add the wine, stock and mushrooms and bring to the boil. Pour into the preheated dish and cover tightly. Bake for 15 minutes. Remove from the oven and give everything a good stir, then return to the oven with the lid on for a further 15 minutes. Check that the liquid has been absorbed and the rice is tender. Stir in the Parmesan, sliced peppers and parsley. Serve sprinkled with extra Parmesan.

Barbecued Stuffed Peppers

Oakhill Potatoes

A bit of a blast from the past — my favourite nurses'-home lunch dish, remembered fondly by hospital staff all over New Zealand. One of the better tasting dishes on the menu.

50 g butter
¼ cup flour
salt and freshly ground black pepper
600 ml milk
2 cups grated tasty cheese
8 medium-sized potatoes, peeled, cooked and sliced
4 hard-boiled eggs, sliced
4–6 rashers bacon, cooked till crispy and
  crumbled or chopped
4 slices toast-cut white bread,
  crusts removed
2 tablespoons chopped parsley

Serves 4–6
Preheat oven to 200°C. Spray a medium-sized lasagne dish with non-stick baking spray.

In a saucepan, melt the butter and stir in the flour using a wire whisk. Cook for 1 minute then season with salt and pepper. Slowly, while whisking, add the milk. Stir until smooth and thickened. Whisk in 1½ cups of the cheese and stir until melted. Do not boil after adding the cheese. Remove from heat.

Layer up the sliced potato, egg and crumbled bacon in the prepared dish and then pour over the cheese sauce. Place the bread slices and remaining ½ cup of cheese in a food processor and whiz into crumbs. Sprinkle over the top of the dish and bake for 25–30 minutes until the crumbs are toasty crisp and the dish heated through. Sprinkle with parsley. This is a lovely supper or lunch dish and nice with a green salad.

6 DESSERTS & GORGEOUS TREATS FOR COFFEE

Gin and Tonic Jellies

150 ml gin
4 teaspoons or 4 sheets gelatine
300 ml lemonade (not diet lemonade)
150 ml tonic (not diet tonic)
1 lemon, sliced thinly, pips removed

Serves 2–4

Pour the gin into a small saucepan and heat until nearly boiling. Remove from heat. Dissolve the gelatine into the gin by stirring with a small whisk. Add the lemonade and tonic and pour into small glasses. Float a lemon slice on top and chill until set.

This can be served with a small scoop of lemon sorbet on top.

A fruity wine version is easy to achieve by using 600 ml of wine to replace the gin, lemonade and tonic, and setting summer berries in the jelly.

Gelatine tips

Powdered gelatine is readily available in supermarkets but it is preferable to use specialised leaf gelatine. Good supermarkets and food stores, delis and kitchen shops sell this. The advantage of leaf gelatine is that it dissolves easily and is clear and flavourless.

One 5 ml teaspoon of gelatine weighs 3 g, one sachet is 10 g.

To use leaf gelatine, soak in cold water for 3–4 minutes, then remove and squeeze out excess water. Drop the leaves into the hot mixture you are preparing to set. Stir until fully dissolved.

One teaspoon (or 3 g) or 1 sheet of gelatine sets 150 ml of liquid.

'Gooey in the Centre' Molten Chocolate Puds

Need I say more?

> 400 g dark chocolate, chopped
> 50 g butter
> ¾ cup caster sugar
> 4 eggs
> 2 tablespoons flour
> softly whipped cream, thick yoghurt or
>   ice cream to serve

Makes 6

Preheat oven to 180°C. Spray 6 cup-sized ramekins or ovenproof coffee cups with non-stick baking spray.

Melt the chocolate — either in a bowl over a saucepan of simmering water, being careful the bowl doesn't actually touch the water; or microwave in short bursts on medium heat, stirring well until melted and smooth.

With an electric mixer, beat the butter and caster sugar together until pale and creamy. Add the eggs, then the melted chocolate and flour. Mix until well combined. Divide the mixture between the prepared ramekins. Place ramekins on an oven tray for ease of handling. Bake for 18–20 minutes. The puddings should be glossy and smooth on top, like a brownie, but soft and gooey in the centre. Don't overcook. Serve with softly whipped cream, thick yoghurt or ice cream.

Frangelico Affogato

Frangelico is an Italian hazelnut liqueur and is quite delicious, but you can easily substitute another liqueur, or omit it altogether for a non-alcoholic version of affogato. (Affogato is Italian for 'drowned', as the ice cream is drowned in coffee.)

8 small scoops vanilla ice cream
(can use a low-fat ice cream)
4 tablespoons Frangelico liqueur
4 cups hot, freshly made espresso coffee

Serves 4

Place 2 small scoops of ice cream in each cup or glass — don't use Granny's best crystal or very fine glass; a more solid beaker, juice glass or coffee cup is best. Pour the Frangelico over the ice cream then pour the hot espresso on top and serve immediately. Give each person a small teaspoon to stir and scoop up the ice cream.

Remember — stressed spelled backwards is desserts.

Butterscotch Banana Saucy Puddings

FOR THE PUDDING
1¼ cups flour
3 teaspoons baking powder
¾ cup caster sugar
1 large or 2 small bananas, mashed with a fork
200 ml milk
100 g butter, melted
1 large egg
1 teaspoon butterscotch or vanilla essence

FOR THE SAUCE
1 cup brown sugar
4 tablespoons golden syrup
1 cup boiling water
½ teaspoon butterscotch or vanilla essence
icing sugar to dust
cream, yoghurt or ice cream to serve

Serve 6

Preheat oven to 180°C. Spray 6 cup-sized ramekins, small bowls or a 2.5 litre pie dish with non-stick baking spray.

Mix all the pudding ingredients in a large bowl with an electric mixer and divide between the prepared bowls.

To make the sauce, mix all ingredients in a large microwave-proof jug and microwave on high until boiling, stirring a couple of times. Carefully pour the boiling mixture over the puddings. Bake for 30–40 minutes. The butterscotch sauce will be all gooey under the sponge. Dust with icing sugar and serve with cream, yoghurt or ice cream.

Coffee Caramel Cream

It is hard to decide which are my favourite desserts — chocolate, lemon or berries — and then of course there are delicious coffee puds. It's so very hard to choose!

3 teaspoons instant coffee powder
2 tablespoons boiling water
1 x 400 g can caramel sweetened condensed milk
250 g cream cheese
1 teaspoon vanilla essence
300 ml cream
extra whipped cream and shaved chocolate or
*   chocolate-coated coffee beans, to serve*

Serves 6

Dissolve the coffee in the boiling water and place in a food processor with the condensed milk, cream cheese and vanilla essence. Mix until well combined. Whip the cream until soft peaks form, then gently fold into the coffee mixture. Serve in wine glasses, Irish coffee glasses or coffee cups, garnished with a little extra whipped cream and shaved chocolate or chocolate-coated coffee beans.

Dark Chocolate Orange Liqueur Mousse

300 ml cream
250 g dark chocolate, chopped
*   (or 1 x 250 g packet dark*
*   chocolate bits or chips)*
3 egg yolks
3 tablespoons orange liqueur, eg Cointreau or
*   Grand Marnier*

Serves 6–8

Heat cream until it is just about to boil. Pour into a blender with the other ingredients. Run the machine until it stops making a racket. Pour mixture into little espresso cups or liqueur glasses and chill overnight, or for at least 3 hours.

This works just as well with milk or white chocolate.

Coffee Caramel Cream

Fanny Gray's Gooseberry Shortcake

My mother is affectionately known as Fanny Gray by her grandchildren. It's a little play on her 'real' name Granny Fay.

250 g butter, softened
1½ cups sugar
2 eggs
1½ cups flour
4 tablespoons cornflour
2 heaped tablespoons custard powder
2 teaspoons baking powder
4-5 cups gooseberries, topped and
    tailed (frozen are fine)
icing sugar to dust
thick yoghurt or softly
    whipped cream to serve

Serves 6

Preheat oven to 200°C. Spray a 23 cm loose-bottomed flan tin, pie dish or spring-form tin with non-stick baking spray.

In an electric mixer, beat the butter and sugar until creamy. Add the eggs, one at a time, then the dry ingredients. Mix until the pastry clumps in a ball around the beater blade. With floured hands, press two-thirds of the pastry into the base and up the sides of the prepared tin — it should be quite sticky. Sprinkle the gooseberries into the tin then roughly roll or press out the remaining pastry to cover the fruit. You can patchwork the pastry to cover any gaps; it doesn't matter if it looks quite raggedy.

Bake for about 20 minutes, then turn the temperature down to 180°C and continue baking for a further 15–20 minutes until the top is evenly golden and crisp. The deeper the fruit, the longer it will take to bake. Cool in the tin and rewarm later to serve. Dust with icing sugar and serve with thick yoghurt or softly whipped cream.

This shortcake recipe works well with other fruits such as apple, blackberries etc.

Raspberry Rhubarb Cinnamon Crumble

2 bunches trimmed rhubarb stalks

3 cups raspberries (if frozen,
   no need to thaw)

1 tablespoon custard powder

½ cup caster sugar

150 g butter, softened and
   cut into cubes

¾ cup flour

1 cup brown sugar

1 cup rolled oats

1 teaspoon cinnamon

icing sugar to dust

thick yoghurt, custard or
   ice cream, to serve

Serves 6

Preheat oven to 170°C. Spray a deep lasagne-type dish or six individual ramekins with non-stick baking spray. Place the chopped rhubarb and raspberries in the prepared dish or dishes. Mix the custard powder and caster sugar and sprinkle over the fruit.

Mix the softened butter, flour, brown sugar, rolled oats and cinnamon, rubbing in the butter to incorporate. Spread the crumble over the fruit and bake for 45–50 minutes, until the fruit is soft and bubbles up through the golden-brown crumble. Dust with icing sugar and serve with thick yoghurt, custard or ice cream.

Sponge Topping for Fruit

Any kind of fruit is good under a quick and easy sponge topping. This recipe can be used as a topping for a large dish, or it will be sufficient for six individual small ramekins or ovenproof noodle-style bowls.

50 g butter, softened

¾ cup sugar

2 eggs

¾ cup milk

1½ cups flour

1 teaspoon baking powder

icing sugar to dust

whipped cream or yoghurt, to serve

Serves 6

Preheat oven to 180°C. Sweeten the fruit of your choice and divide between the dishes. Beat the butter and sugar until light and fluffy. Add the eggs, one at a time, mixing well after each addition. Add the milk, flour and baking powder.

Divide the topping mixture between the six dishes. Place the dishes in a large roasting dish to catch any overflow. Bake for 30 minutes until the sponge is golden brown. Dust with icing sugar to serve and pass around softly whipped cream or yoghurt to accompany.

Raspberry Rhubarb Cinnamon Crumble

Chocolate, Prune and Almond Meringue Cake

2 cups whole almonds,
  blanched if you prefer
300 g chocolate
6 egg whites
2 cups caster sugar
1 cup chopped, pitted prunes
250 ml cream
extra chopped chocolate and
  sliced almonds for sprinkling

Serves 10

Preheat oven to 160°C. Spray a large 25 cm spring-form tin with non-stick baking spray and line with baking paper.

Chop the whole almonds in a food processor or with a knife until quite fine — like coarse breadcrumbs. Chop the chocolate roughly, either in a food processor or with a knife.

In a separate bowl, beat the egg whites until really stiff. Add the caster sugar slowly, a teaspoon at a time, until the mixture is thick and glossy. Fold through the chopped almonds, chocolate and prunes. Spoon the mixture into the prepared tin and bake for 1½ hours. Cool in the tin, then release and place on a serving plate.

Whip the cream and spread generously over the top. Sprinkle with extra chopped chocolate and sliced almonds. Keep chilled until serving time. This makes a great birthday dessert.

Melon and Berries with Lemongrass Syrup

1 cup orange juice
½ cup caster sugar
2 stalks of lemongrass (the white parts only),
    chopped and bruised
1 cup water
½ rock melon or honeydew melon, deseeded
an equal quantity of watermelon, deseeded
1 punnet strawberries, hulled and halved
1 cup blueberries
1 cup raspberries
mint leaves to garnish

Serves 4–6

Place the orange juice, caster sugar, lemongrass and water in a small saucepan. Bring to the boil, stirring until the sugar dissolves. Boil gently for 5 minutes, then cool. When completely cold, strain to remove the lemongrass.

Using a melon baller, cut little balls from the rock melon and watermelon. If you don't have a baller, cut into small pieces. Place the melon and berries in a bowl and drizzle the syrup over. Garnish with mint leaves.

Sticky Gingerbread with Crème Fraîche and Crystallised Ginger

This makes a large cake or two smaller loaves. It is handy to freeze for another occasion or it can be treated as or loaf and sliced and buttered. A very versatile recipe for ginger lovers.

100 g butter, softened but not melted

¾ cup sugar

2 eggs

1 cup golden syrup

1½ cups milk

2 teaspoons baking soda

3½ cups flour

2 tablespoons ground ginger
  (yes, that is tablespoons!)

½ cup finely sliced or
  chopped crystallised ginger

crème fraîche, whipped cream, slices of
  crystallised ginger or maple syrup to serve

Makes at least 10 portions

Preheat oven to 160°C. Spray and line a 23 cm square cake tin or 2 standard loaf tins with non-stick baking spray and baking paper.

Beat the butter and sugar until creamy. Add the eggs one at a time and beat until fluffy. Add the golden syrup (standing the tin in hot water will make it easier to pour into the measuring cup). Warm the milk by microwaving for 40 seconds, then stir in the soda. Add this and the flour to the mixture, alternating between the two and continuing to beat. Add the ground ginger and chopped crystallised ginger. Pour into the prepared tin or tins.

Bake the large cake for 1½ hours, testing to see the cake has pulled away from the edges of the tin and is firm in the middle. The two loaves will take approximately 1 hour to cook. Cool in the tins for 30 minutes before cooling further on a wire rack.

Serve a wedge or chunky slice, warmed in the microwave, with crème fraîche or whipped cream, a few slices of crystallised ginger and a drizzle of maple syrup if desired.

Lemon Posset

This is my favourite old-fashioned English creamy citrus dessert. I use it a lot when I have to feed a large number of people and need to be well organised in advance. It can be ready and waiting in the fridge a couple of days ahead if need be.

600 ml cream
¾ cup caster sugar
grated rind and juice of 2 lemons
whipped cream, lemon curd or grated lemon rind to serve

Makes 10–12 servings in small glasses

Place the cream and caster sugar in a small saucepan and stir as it comes to the boil. Once it boils, reduce the heat to keep gently boiling and time the mixture for exactly 3 minutes. This timing is very important to the 'chemistry' of the recipe. Remove from the heat and whisk in the grated rind and lemon juice. Cool, then pour into small glasses (sherry or liqueur glasses are ideal). Chill for at least 6–8 hours, or it's even better if you can make it the night before. Serve chilled with a small dollop of softly whipped cream or lemon curd and a sprinkle of grated lemon rind over the top. Alternatively, serve with thick lemon yoghurt.

Homemade Hokey Pokey Ice Cream

½ cup brown sugar
2 tablespoons golden syrup
1 teaspoon baking soda
1 x 400 g can sweetened condensed milk
450 ml cream, whipped
150 ml milk

Serves 4–6

Melt the brown sugar and golden syrup together, then carefully boil for 4 timed minutes. Stir to prevent catching on the pan. Stir in the baking soda and pour out onto a sheet of non-stick baking paper to set.

When set, smash and crush the hokey pokey into pieces. In a large mixer bowl, mix the condensed milk, whipped cream and milk. Add the crushed hokey pokey and freeze in an ice cream machine. Alternatively, freeze in a plastic container but stir 2 to 3 times in the first hour of freezing to break up the ice crystals.

Pear and White Spice Sorbet

There's real fire-and-ice combination in this easy and clever recipe.

2 x 400 g cans pear halves in syrup, sliced
   (note that they need to be in syrup not
   juice for this recipe to work)
4 poached baby pears or canned pear halves
¼ teaspoon ground white pepper
¼ teaspoon ground allspice

Serves 4

At least a day before serving, remove the lids and labels from the 2 cans of pears in syrup and freeze until solid. You can keep a couple of cans in the freezer on stand-by for a speedy dessert. You can try canned apricots or peaches too.

About 10 minutes before serving, get four cocktail or wine glasses. Drain the four poached pears or pear halves. Remove the frozen pears from the freezer and run the can under hot water to loosen the edges. Place the solid lumps of pear in the bowl of a food processor and chop up roughly with a knife. Add the white pepper and allspice and run the machine to purée the pears into a slushy mush. Spoon into glasses and top with a baby pear or pear half. Serve immediately.

Homemade Hokey Pokey Ice Cream

It's not just about food — it's the whole social ritual of dining that I love so much. Sharing meals with people is a great way to break down barriers.

Lemon Coconut Tart

The quickest, easiest pudding imaginable.

1 tablespoon grated lemon rind
100 ml fresh lemon juice
1 cup caster sugar
4 eggs
1 cup desiccated coconut
125 g butter, softened
1 cup cream
½ cup coconut cream
½ cup flour
icing sugar to dust
whipped cream and fresh berries to serve

Serves 4–6

Preheat oven to 180°C. Spray a 21–23 cm cake tin with non-stick baking spray and line the base with baking paper.

Place all the ingredients, except the icing sugar, cream and berries, in a blender and process until smooth. Pour into the prepared tin and bake for 45–50 minutes. Cover with a sheet of tinfoil if the surface is getting too brown. Cool in the tin then refrigerate. Dust with icing sugar and serve with softly whipped cream and fresh berries.

Cooking should be fun — make it easy for yourself.

Simon's Berry Mousse Cake

This is really a version of a cheesecake but our young builder friend, Simon, who was chief tester at recipe-development time, said 'I really love the topping and think you should ditch the base' — so that's how it came to be.

750 g cream cheese, at room temperature
1 cup caster sugar
2 cups cream
3 teaspoons raspberry jelly crystals
¼ cup boiling water
1 cup raspberries
1 cup blackberries
1 cup blueberries
1 cup boysenberries (or 4 cups of any
   combination of berries — frozen are fine,
   no need to thaw)
extra berries and 1 cup raspberry jam to garnish

Serves 6–8

Spray a large 28–30 cm spring-form tin with non-stick baking spray, then line the base and sides with baking paper. Lining the sides is easy to do by cutting a long strip about 15 cm wide and sticking it onto the baking spray. The collar should reach higher than the metal side.

Beat the cream cheese and caster sugar together until well combined. Add the cream. Dissolve the jelly in the boiling water and add to the cream cheese mix. Beat until thick and smooth and well combined. Fold through the berries —just lightly mix them in — then pour into the prepared tin. Freeze until set (at least 3 hours).

To serve, cover the top with berries and pour the jam over them. Use a knife, run under hot water, to slice into wedges. Wipe the knife after each cut.

Jo's Fabulous Fudge

If you like a smooth, creamy, luxurious fudge that is not at all sugary or hard, and is easy to cut into portions without crumbling, then this is the one. It should definitely not be part of the daily diet — to be made for special occasions only.

2 x 400 g cans sweetened condensed milk
2 cups firmly packed brown sugar
250 g butter
100 ml liquid glucose syrup (available in
    the baking section of a good supermarket,
    or from a pharmacy. Corn syrup can
    be substituted)

3 tablespoons golden syrup
400 g white (or milk or dark)
    chocolate, chopped
1 teaspoon vanilla essence

Makes about 60 pieces

Take a 20 x 30 cm tin that's at least 4 cm deep (or 2 smaller tins), spray with non-stick baking spray and line with non-stick baking paper.

Place all the ingredients, except the chocolate and vanilla essence, in a large, heavy-based saucepan and stir over a medium heat until the butter melts and the sugar dissolves. Bring to the boil and boil gently until the mixture becomes very thick and changes colour to a dark caramel shade — about 6 minutes (116°C or soft-ball stage on a sugar thermometer). Stir continually to prevent it catching on the bottom (I find a silicon spatula the best gadget to stir this with). Remove from heat and stand until the bubbles subside. Stir in the chocolate and vanilla essence until melted and smooth.

Pour into the prepared tin and smooth the surface. Cool to room temperature (about 3 hours), then refrigerate until firm. Cut into squares. This will keep in an airtight container in the fridge for up to 6 weeks — if no one finds it first!

Fairy Mushrooms

An unashamedly nostalgic treat for children and adults alike.

*12 fruit stick sweets, purchased from
  the local dairy
24 soft marshmallows, pink and white
1 cup chocolate melts or buttons,
  melted in the microwave
½ cup coconut*

Makes 24

Cut the fruit sticks in half and poke them into the marshmallows. Dip into the melted chocolate then into the coconut. Allow to set on a sheet of tinfoil. Store in an airtight glass jar.

Granny Win's Sago Cream

Granny Winifred Matson is my maternal grandmother and this is her recipe. It was a childhood favourite that I've re-invented as a smart dinner-party dessert.

*4 tablespoons sago
1200 ml full-cream milk
3 eggs, separated
2 tablespoons sugar*

*¼ tablespoon salt
1 teaspoon vanilla essence
whipped cream or crème fraîche
  and fruit, to serve (optional)*

Serves 6

Soak the sago in milk for 15 minutes. In a double-boiler saucepan, cook over medium heat, stirring until the sago is quite transparent. This will take about 20 minutes.

Beat the egg yolks, sugar and salt until pale and thick. Add the vanilla essence. Whisk into the sago mixture in the double boiler and stir until creamy and custard-like. Cool to room temperature.

Beat the egg whites until stiff and fold into the sago. Serve in wine or parfait glasses with a little softly whipped cream or crème fraîche and fruit if desired.

Fairy Mushrooms

Tuile Bowls

These are handy as they can be used to really smarten up a simple dessert of ice cream, sorbets or fruit into something extra-special.

125 g butter	1 cup flour
½ cup caster sugar	pinch salt
3 tablespoons brown sugar	1 teaspoon vanilla essence
4 egg whites	

Makes 6 bowls

Preheat oven to 180°C. Lay a sheet of baking paper or a silicon mat on a baking tray.

Using an electric mixer, beat the butter and both sugars together until creamy and fluffy. Add the egg whites, one at a time, then mix in the flour, salt and vanilla essence.

Ladle two heaped tablespoons of the mixture onto the prepared baking tray and spread out to the size of a bread-and-butter plate or large saucer (about 15 cm). If possible, make the edges slightly thicker than the centre for even cooking. Bake for 8–10 minutes, checking to see if it is cooking evenly. You may have to rotate the tray. Lift the tuile off the tray and press into a small noodle bowl to mould into a cup shape. Press the bottom down to flatten. Cool until firm and crisp in the bowl, then transfer to a wire rack. Repeat with the remaining mixture.Note: if the tuiles cool too quickly to shape, return them to the oven for a minute to soften and start again.

Cheat's Liquorice Icecream

6 pieces of soft liquorice pipe, cut into approximately 1 cup of small pieces (I use a brown paper bag of liquorice from the supermarket)	2 litres of vanilla ice cream (can be low fat) extra liquorice or liquorice allsorts to garnish

Serves 8

Soak the liquorice pieces overnight, or for at least 6 hours, in enough cold water to cover. Soften the ice cream at room temperature. Spoon half of it into a food processor. Add the drained liquorice, which should be quite pulpy and soft. Run the machine to blend thoroughly, then stir this back into the remaining ice cream. The colour is quite an unfortunate khaki, but the taste is divine. Refreeze the ice cream until required. This will keep in the freezer for 3–4 weeks. Serve in small bowls or parfait dishes with liquorice pieces to garnish (liquorice allsorts are also good decorations).

Tuile Bowls

Milk Chocolate, Coconut and Raisin Slice

450 g milk chocolate
1½ cups soft, sticky seedless raisins
4 eggs
¾ cup sugar
1½ cups desiccated coconut

Makes 24–28 squares

Spray a 20 x 30 cm sponge-roll tin with non-stick baking spray and line with baking paper.

Melt the chocolate, either in the microwave or in a bowl over hot water. Pour into the base of the prepared tin and smooth out to cover the base evenly. Allow to cool and harden — in the fridge is good.

Preheat oven to 180°C.

Sprinkle raisins over the set chocolate base. Beat the eggs in a bowl with an electric mixer. Add the sugar and beat well, then add the coconut. Mix until well combined. Spoon this mixture evenly over the raisins, pressing down gently to smooth the surface. Bake for 25–30 minutes until the coconut topping is golden brown and feels quite firm to touch. Leave to cool in the tin.

Mark into squares after 30 minutes, then allow to set solid. Place in the refrigerator for 1 hour until the slice is completely cold, then cut into pieces down the scored lines.

Live well,
love much,
laugh often.

Deb's Peppermint Chocolate Slice

My friend Deb has made this special treat for years. She gave me the recipe and it is now part of our family's folklore, affectionately known as 'Deb's peppermint stuff'.

FOR THE BASE
125 g butter
3 tablespoons cocoa
½ cup caster sugar
1 egg
1 teaspoon vanilla essence
1 cup desiccated coconut
½ cup chopped walnuts
2 cups biscuit crumbs
    (wine, digestive etc)

FOR THE MIDDLE LAYER
4 tablespoons Kremelta (melted)
4 tablespoons milk
2 cups icing sugar
2 teaspoons peppermint essence

FOR THE TOPPING
50 g butter
250 g dark chocolate melts or
    chocolate chips

Makes 40 pieces

Spray a 20 x 30 cm sponge-roll tin with non-stick baking spray and line with baking paper.

In a small saucepan combine the butter, cocoa and caster sugar and stir over a gentle heat until the sugar is dissolved. Remove from heat and beat in the egg and vanilla essence, then mix in the coconut, walnuts and biscuit crumbs and press into the prepared tin. Chill.

Mix the middle-layer ingredients until smooth and spread over the chilled base.

To make the topping, melt the butter and chocolate together until smooth, then spread over the chilled slice. Return to the fridge, then cut into pieces when cold.

This slice can be stored in an airtight tin but is especially good if served cold from the fridge. Wonderful with coffee in lieu of dessert.

White Chocolate Raspberry Truffles

1 punnet (approximately 2 cups) fresh raspberries
1 x 395 g packet white chocolate melts

Makes 50

Pick over the raspberries, discarding any less-than-perfect specimens. They should be quite firm and dry. Place the selected fruit on a small tray and chill in the fridge for 1 hour, or in the freezer for 15 minutes.

Melt the white chocolate according to the packet instructions. I find white chocolate is best gently coaxed into melting by placing in a bowl over, but not touching, simmering water. Stir gently to make smooth.

Using a chocolate-dipping fork or skewer, dunk the raspberries into the chocolate, then place them onto a sheet of non-stick baking paper or tinfoil to set completely. Keep cool before serving, but not in the fridge as chocolate tends to sweat when refrigerated.

This recipe works equally well with dark or milk chocolate.

Cinnamon, Fig and Walnut Salami

These logs make a wonderful gift and are great sliced to serve with coffee.

2 cups dried figs, chopped
1 cup pitted dates, chopped
1 cup seedless raisins
2 teaspoons ground cinnamon
2 teaspoons vanilla essence
1 cup chocolate chips or
  chopped dark chocolate
1 cup whole walnuts
1 cup icing sugar

Makes 3 rolls

Place figs, dates, raisins, walnuts, cinnamon, vanilla essence and chocolate chips in a food processor. Run the machine to process into a thick, gooey paste that clumps together around the food processor blade. Add the whole walnuts. Divide the mixture in half. Place a sheet of non-stick baking paper on the bench and dredge with icing sugar. Place a portion of the mixture onto the icing sugar and, using the paper, roll up into a thick salami sausage roll. Wrap securely in a fresh piece of baking paper and store in the fridge. Repeat with the remaining portions. Slice into thin discs to serve.

Weights & Measures Conversion Tables

Temperature

Celcius	Fahrenheit	Oven
110	225	Cool
130	250	Cool
140	275	Cool
150	300	Low
180	350	Moderate
200	400	Hot
220	425	Hot
230	450	Very Hot

Volume

1 cup	250 ml
1 tablespoon	15 ml
1 dessertspoon	10 ml
1 teaspoon	5 ml

Weights

plain and self-raising flour	1 cup	150 g
white sugar	1 cup	225 g
caster sugar	1 cup	220 g
brown sugar (tightly packed)	1 cup	200 g
brown sugar (lightly packed)	1 cup	160 g
icing sugar	1 cup	150 g
couscous	1 cup	180 g
rice — basmati, jasmine, long-grain	1 cup	200 g
rice — arborio	1 cup	220 g
grated cheese	1 cup	100 g
butter (one American stick)	8 tbsp	100 g

Volume

¼ tsp		1.25 ml
½ tsp		2.5 ml
1 tsp		5 ml
1 tbs		15 ml
1 fl oz		30 ml
2 fl oz		50 ml
5 fl oz	½ pint	150 ml
7 fl oz	⅓ pint	200 ml
10 fl oz	½ pint	300 ml
15 fl oz	¾ pint	425 ml
20 fl oz	1 pint	600 ml
	1 ¼ pints	700 ml
	1 ½ pints	850 ml
	1 ¾ pints	1 litre
	2 pints	1.2 litres
	3 ½ pints	2 litres

Weight

10 g	½ oz
20 g	¾ oz
25 g	1 oz
50 g	2 oz
75 g	3 oz
110 g	4 oz
150 g	5 oz
175 g	6 oz
200 g	7 oz
225 g	8 oz
250 g	9 oz
275 g	9 ½ oz
300 g	10 ½ oz
350 g	12 oz
375 g	13 oz
400 g	14 oz
425 g	15 oz
450 g	1 lb
700 g	1 ½ lb
750 g	1 lb 10 oz
1 kg	2 ¼ lb
1.25 kg	2 lb 12 oz
1.5 kg	3 lb 5 oz
2 kg	4 ½ lb
2.25 kg	5 lb
2.5 kg	5 lb 8 oz
3 kg	6 lb 8 oz

Seagars at Oxford

In June 2006, Jo Seagar opened her new cook school, café and kitchen store in Oxford, a small town in North Canterbury about 45 minutes from central Christchurch.

The cook school is a hands-on experience, running class for for 8 to 12 people at a time, followed by lunch in the private dining room. As Jo points out, the food is an excuse for fun and friendship.

Taking pride of place at the cook school is a large Aga oven. Jo has dreamed of owning one of these for many years and she is very keen to proudly show it off.

The café is a relaxed space serving an all-day brunch and lunch menu. The emphasis is on casual but knowledgeable service.

The kitchen store is stocked with items that Jo has selected as the best available. This includes state-of-the-art KitchenAid or Magimix appliances and accessories — or a simple yet highly functional plastic potato peeler.

For more information contact Jo at Seagars at Oxford, PO Box 42, Oxford 7443, New Zealand.
Email: jo@joseagar.com
Websites: www.joseagar.com
www.seagarsatoxford.com

Index